MEDIEVAL CALLIGRAPHY:

A MODERN PRIMER

By:

Jason L. Parish

Cover Photo: Parish, J. (2006) *Magnificat* [gouache, ink, and 23k gold leaf on vellum], Personal Collection.

Table of Contents

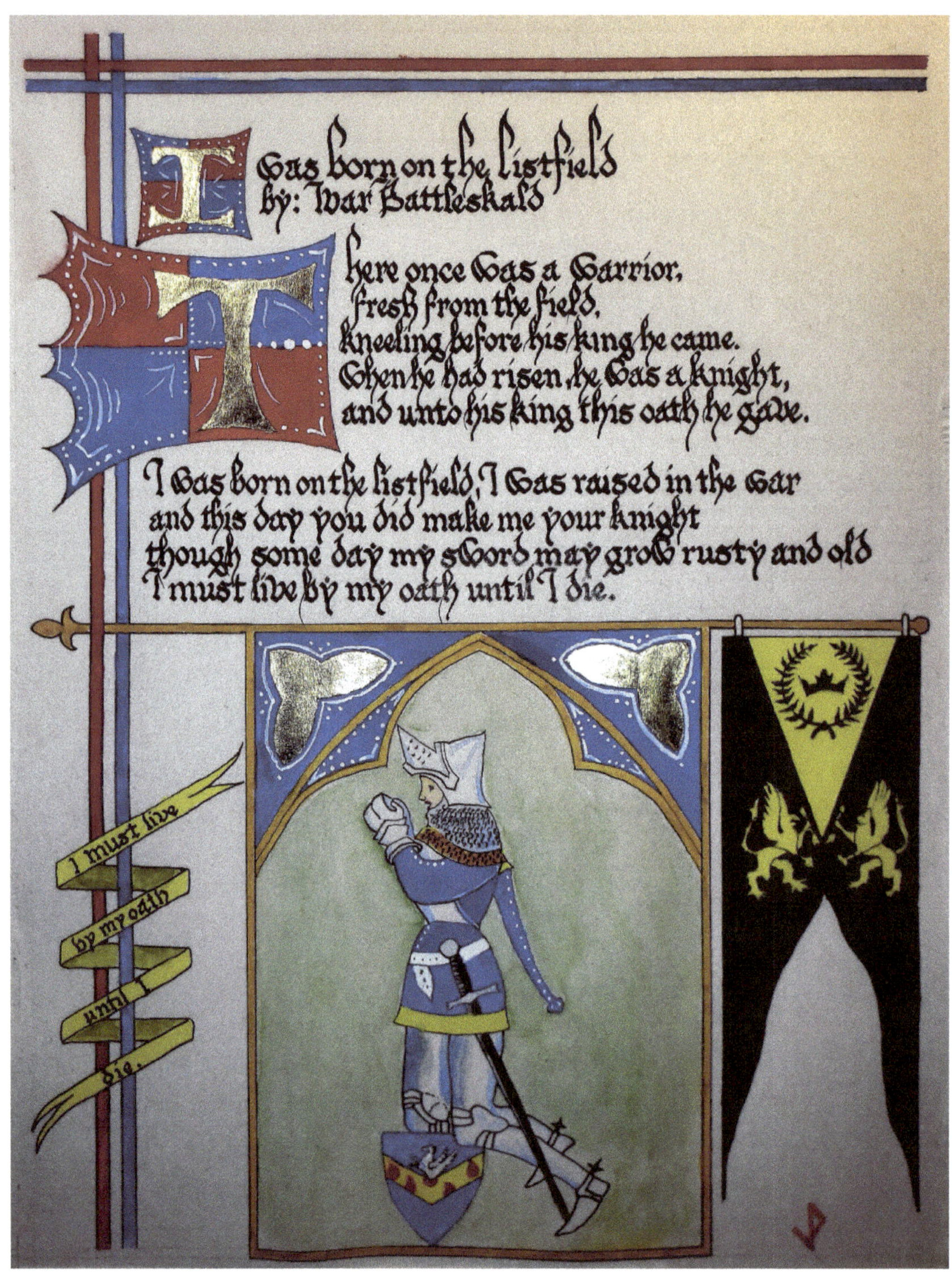

TABLE OF FIGURES

ACKNOWLEDGEMENTS

First and foremost, I must give my undying thanks to my wife, Jennifer. Her continuous encouragement, understanding, and patience have been a priceless gift. Her ability to withstand my incessant blathering on about trivial scribal minutiae without rolling her eyes and throttling me is most impressive.

My children, Bridgette and Malcolm, have also been vital to this project. Over the years they have endured their roles as calligraphic guinea pigs with stoic calm.

Thanks also to two great teachers who inspired me to study art and art history more broadly: Sallie Bowen-Ulsher and Brad Loewen.

Finally, thanks to several members of the Society for Creative Anachronism who have been instrumental in my development as an artisan, a scribe, and a human in general: Jacquie Ziegler, Jennifer Kirts Hansen, and Sean Oppenheimer.

PREFACE

Calligraphy, or the art of writing beautifully, is an immensely rewarding activity. You may choose to study and practice it for personal satisfaction, artistic expression, or even professional occupation. Some of us use it as a way to connect to the past through historic reenactment groups such as the Society for Creative Anachronism (www.sca.org).

I have been a calligrapher since 1985 when I took it up to help improve my then chicken-scratch like handwriting. I become a medieval reenactor in 1992 and I was ecstatic to discover that the awards given were all done in the medieval styles I had been ogling in various historic manuscript reproductions. I was hooked immediately and have remained so since. Within the Arts & Sciences area of the SCA, I have focused largely on calligraphy, illumination, and the production/manufacture of the various inks, pigments, and binders used throughout the early to late middle ages.

Throughout the early years of my scribal formation, I was predominantly self-taught. One of the great frustrations I experienced as an autodidact was the dearth of clearly written instructions with illustrations or photographs which plainly reflected the machinations of the hand while in motion. I am very much a visual learner and prefer to see all the nuances of movement in order to accomplish a task.

I began teaching calligraphy & Illumination in 2005 with the encouragement of several friends who knew of my love and desire to share the scribal arts. I have since taught hundreds of students through classes, one-on-one instruction, and instructional videos. This book is the culmination of my class notes, experiments, and student feedback.

My hope for me is to create a usable textbook for both the solitary practitioner as well as the classroom environment. You can learn in a vacuum, but it sure is more fun to have a group with whom to laugh, learn, and lean-on. My hope for you, dear student, is simply to learn to relax, have fun, and enjoy the process of creating art.

INTRODUCTION

As we begin our study of calligraphy in general, and medieval calligraphy specifically, we will examine the medieval tools and materials that were in use between, roughly 476 CE through 1603 CE. This date range considers the Early, Middle, and Late Middle Ages as well as the Renaissance. We will compare those tools and materials with their modern equivalents.

Once we have become accustomed to using pen, ink, and paper, we will begin to add some form to our scribbles. While every individual hand (or 'font,' if you will) has its own unique stroke vocabulary, there are some pen strokes that are fundamental to writing in general. You will begin to learn proper body position, breathing technique, and stroke technique through a series of exercises. These exercises are very useful as you proceed with your studies as they help to limber up the hand and arm in preparation to write.

Next, we will work on several different hands that were commonly used through the period. Be forewarned: this is not an exhaustive study of all the hands and variants used throughout all of Europe during this time period. We will instead be focusing on three: Uncial Majuscule, Carolingian Miniscule, and Gothic Textura Quadrata. Within this set, you will find sufficient variety to fulfill most any project and develop the foundational skills to learn other similar hands.

Within each calligraphic hand study, you will find multiple small projects intended to help sharpen your skills. I would encourage you to keep these projects tucked away someplace safe. Come back to them after you have spent at least a full year practicing and try the projects once more. Now, compare the results! You will no doubt be flabbergasted at the progress you have made.

In the appendices, you will find a list of art supply dealers. I encourage you to shop at local brick and mortar stores where possible. When that isn't possible, please choose reputable dealers with a good reputation for positive customer service.

In the last appendix, you will find practice sheets for your convenience. DON'T WRITE ON THEM, you silly goose! Photocopy first, then practice. This insures their continued availability.

As a note, this is obviously not a comprehensive collection of medieval calligraphic hands. It is only a primer intended to give you the best possible start in the practice of medieval style calligraphy. If the nuances of paleography intrigue you, there are plenty of terrific sources which are easily located and procured. For a more in-depth study of any of the historical writing systems and the evolution of calligraphic styles, look at a few of the titles in the references section. They will provide you with a solid foundation and guidance to proceed from there.

I think it is time for us to get to work. Make yourself a cup of tea, get comfortable, and let's have a go! This will be a grand adventure, indeed.

I. TOOLS AND MATERIALS

Any trip to your average well-stocked art supply store can be overwhelming to say the least. For many of us addicts, that same trip can lead to severe trauma to the bank account as well. Having a game plan and a shopping list before you go can help save you money, storage space, and sanity. Educating yourself ahead of time is essential. Look online, read reviews, and don't be afraid to ask questions. This is your hard-earned money we're talking about and life is simply too short to use inferior tools and materials.

Calligraphy, at its most basic form, requires only some tool to make marks with and a surface upon which to make those marks. A stick can readily inscribe letters in wet sand at the beach. Most of us, I think, would prefer to focus on writing with pen and ink for the time being. I'll leave you to write dirty limericks on lakeshores on your own time.

Let's look at some of the basic items of kit that you will need. These are my recommendations for starting out. The important thing is to experiment. Find what works the best for you. I can only give you my opinions based on my knowledge and experience. Ultimately, however, what may work well for me may not work for you. Give yourself permission to play. Go ahead, do it!

Pens, Nibs, and Nib Holders

Pens, pens, glorious pens! There are so many options to choose from that it can be bewildering. As a novice, you will want something convenient, easy to use, and, frankly, inexpensive. I highly recommend starting off with one of the felt-tip markers described below. They allow you to begin practice immediately, concentrate on your letter formation, and not worry about managing ink flow. Your experience may, of course, vary, but my students have made faster improvement while practicing with markers than when using traditional dip-pens.

Quill Pens

In Europe in the middle ages, the goose quill was the primary writing instrument; specifically, the primary wing feathers taken from the left side of the bird. (As writing with one's left hand was discouraged during this time, this guidance is directed mainly towards righthanders.) The curve in these 'sinister' quills would arc over the back of the right hand and thus out of the line of sight.

Goose feathers, along with those of swan, crow, and other large birds, would be stripped of their barbs and cut down to 7 or so inches in length. Their tips would be tempered in hot sand or simply allowed to age and dry naturally. They would then be cut to shape and split with a very sharp, small-bladed penknife. Pith, if any remained, was removed and the hollow stem of the quills functioned as reservoirs. The quills relied on capillary action to feed the tines through the split. When the tip became dull or broke, the quill was simply dressed back to a fresh edge. They could be recut and reused until there was very little remaining.

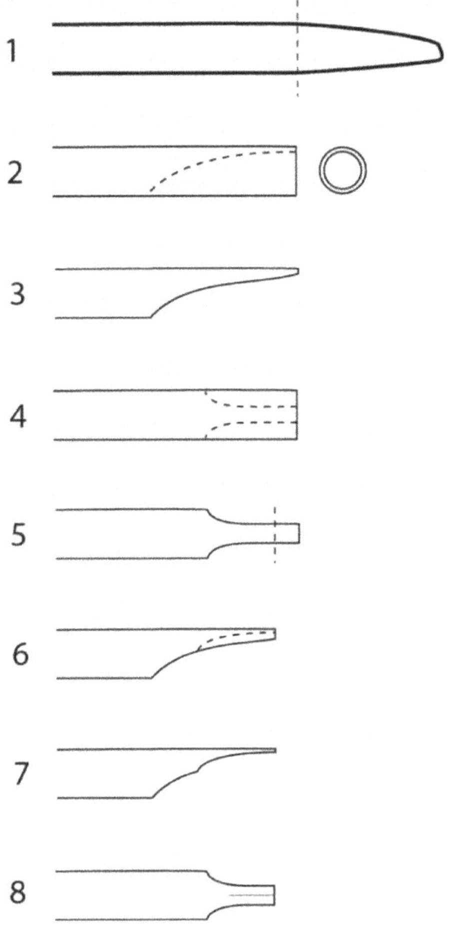

Figure 1 - Cutting a Quill Pen

1. After the feather has been stripped and tempered in hot sand, it is cut square at the end.

2. A cut is made, sweeping towards the opposite edge.

3. Any remaining pith is removed, and the cut is faired.

4. The shoulders are cut, forming the chisel edge.

5. The quill is cut to length.

6. Additional material is removed to provide flexibility to the pen.

7. The tip can be scraped thinner if desired.

8. The quill is split and the shape and size are finalized.

Quill pens, while initially cumbersome and time-consuming to work with, have an elasticity unmatched by any other material. Also, it is possible to obtain extremely fine lines in lettering with the use of a properly cut and maintained quill that is difficult to attain when using steel nibs. Give yourself time to get used to writing with a dip pen before you tackle the quill-pen. There's a learning curve to them that can be largely mitigated by mastering steel nibs first. Afterwards, you may find that you prefer writing with a goose feather over any other pen in your collection.

Markers

As I have mentioned previously, I am an ardent proponent of using felt-tip calligraphy markers in practice sessions. Speedball, Staedtler, Itoya, Faber-Castell, and others produce them in a variety of colors and tip sizes (See Figures 1 and 2). Some even come double-tipped; giving you access to two different sizes of pen in a single package. Aside from their convenience, another advantage that I find appealing is that markers can be used on regular printer paper and grid paper without bleeding through or running.

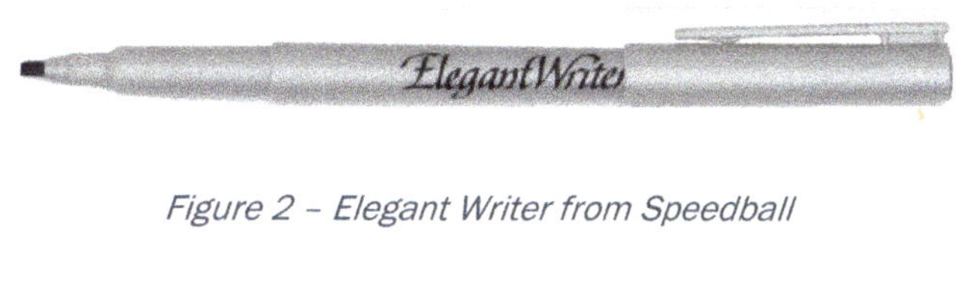

Figure 2 – Elegant Writer from Speedball

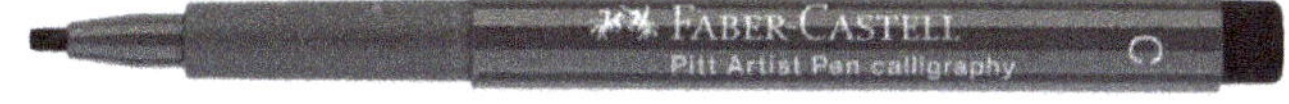

Figure 3 – Faber-Castell Pitt Artist Pen

I am not, however, keen on their use in finished pieces meant to be kept for long periods of time or displayed. That being said, there are some on the market which are Ph-neutral, lightfast, and archival, which are advantageous qualities for art conservation. Unfortunately, the semi-translucent quality of the ink application when using markers diminishes the visual appeal for me. For a final product, I prefer an opaque, dense ink or gouache application.

Fountain and Cartridge Pens

Both fountain and cartridge pens usually feature a replaceable nib. Fountain pens have a flexible bladder inside the body of the pen, which is filled by means of a lever which compresses the reservoir. Cartridge pens feature a removable, small, plastic cylinder which can be either of a disposable or a permanent nature. The price and quality vary according to the manufacturer and can range from $5 to several thousand dollars.

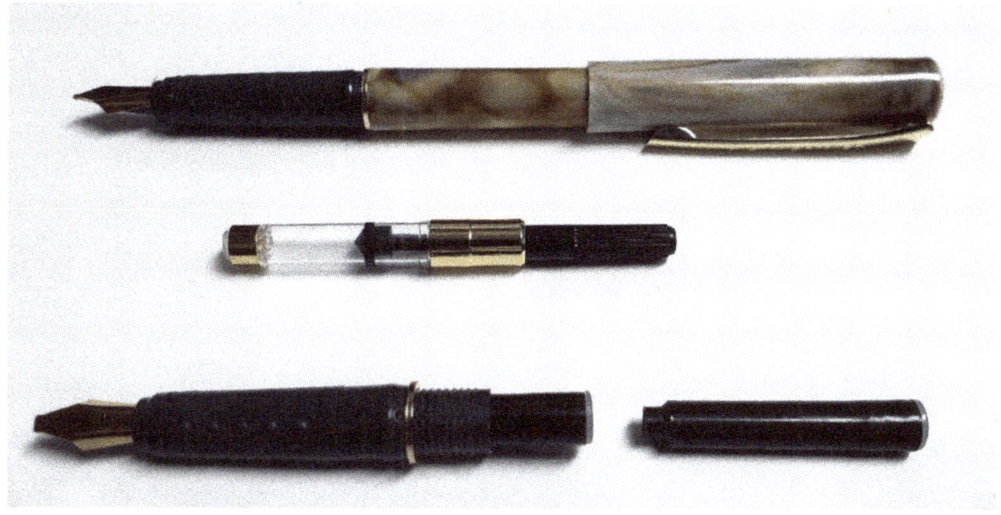

Figure 4 - Staedtler Cartridge Pen, Disposable Cartridges, and Refillable Piston Cartridge

Fountain and cartridge pens are mixed blessings. On one hand, they offer convenience, easy ink flow, and decent fine line production. On the other hand, the ink can be splotchy and tends to run and bleed, the pens can clog or dry out and require regular maintenance. Changing nibs and ink colors can also be troublesome and messy.

Schaeffer, Osmiroid, Speedball, and Pilot (among many others) make excellent pens. You will generally get what you pay for, up to a certain point. Look online and drool at the high-end goodies. I will let you, your wallet, and your significant other help you to determine where you draw the line. I would dissuade you from using this style of pen until you have spent a fair measure of time mastering basic techniques using a marker.

Dip Pens

More commonly called a nib and nib-holder, this is the standard workhorse of the serious calligrapher. It consists of, surprisingly, a nib – a steel or brass writing tip with a reservoir clip – and a handle called a nib-holder. Nib-holders can be found as simple, cheap plastic handles (See Figure 3) all the way up to exotic turned-wood pieces of art. I prefer a common wooden model that has a cork grip (See Figure 4). They're comfortable, inexpensive, and readily available.

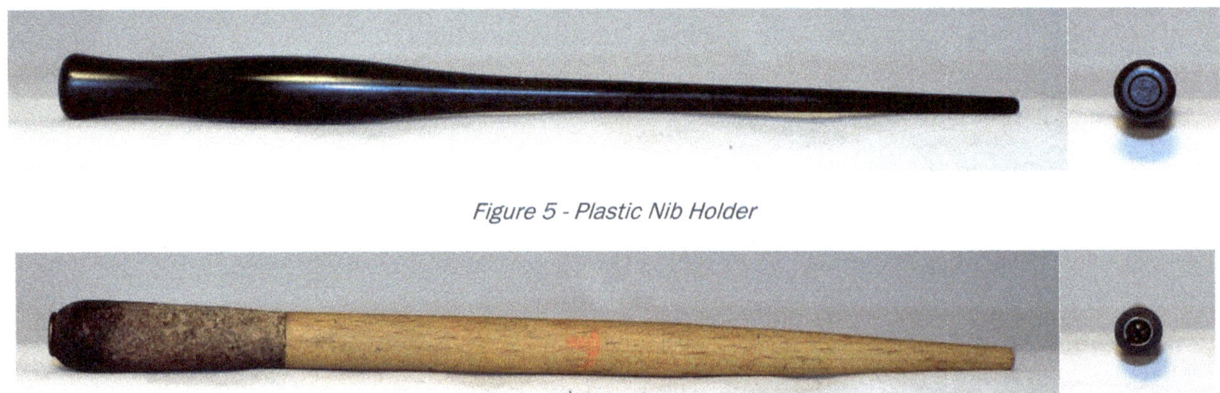

Figure 5 - Plastic Nib Holder

Figure 6 - Wood and Cork Nib Holder

Nibs come in a bewildering array of sizes, offsets, brands, and types. For now, we are going to focus only on the broad- or chisel-edge nibs which emulate the quill pen. Speedball/Hunt, Mitchell, and Brause are commonly available nibs with Brause being my preference overall.

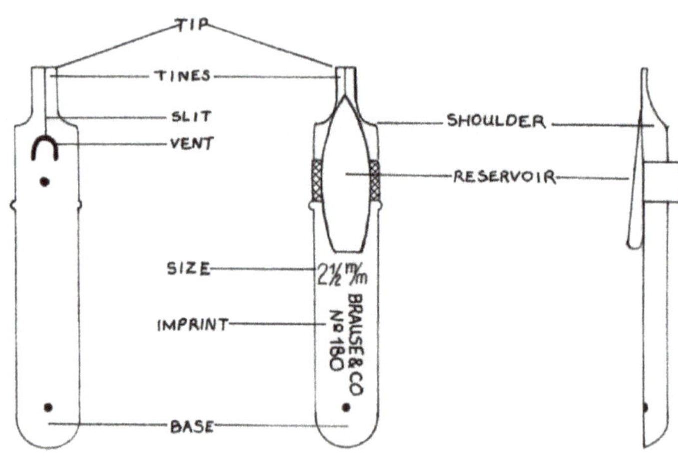

Figure 7 - Brause Nib Anatomy

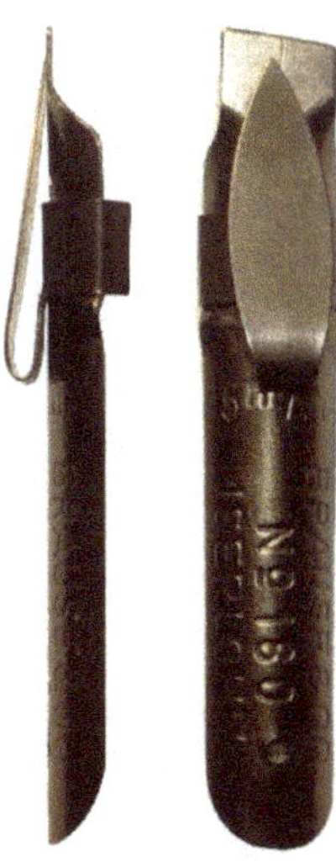

Figure 8 - Brause Nib Side and Top Views

To fill and use a nib, begin by choosing the size you need and your favorite holder. I like to hold the nib in a folded section of paper towel or a chamois cloth to prevent transferring body oils to the nib then insert the base firmly into the holder. While you can dip the nib into a bottle of ink to load it, I find that this is extremely messy. If it is your preference to do so, just make sure to wipe off the pen before writing.

I like to load my nibs by using the dropper that is common in many ink bottles or a fine glass eyedropper. This is accomplished by squeezing the dropper's bulb and releasing it a couple times to mix the ink and fill the bulb and pipette. Then position the tip of the dropper against the side of the nib reservoir and gently squeeze. You should see the ink filling the space. Replace the dropper into the bottle, screw it back in place, and you are ready to write.

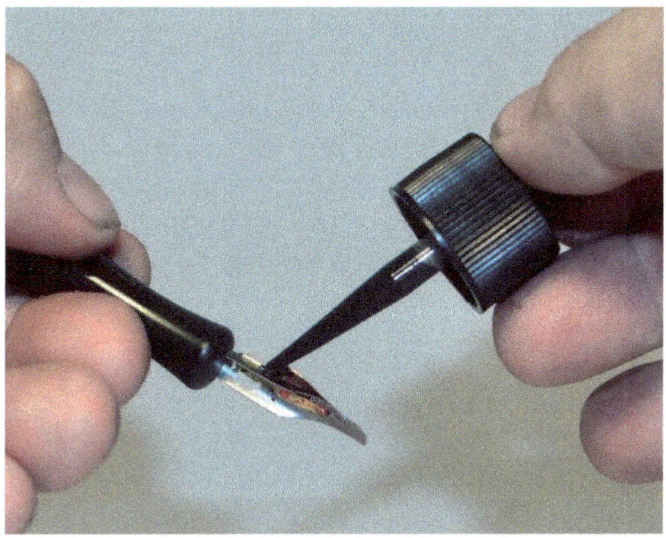

Figure 9 - Loading a Nib with Ink

However you load the nib, you will frequently have to coax the ink to flow. I will keep a scrap of paper nearby, preferably of the type being used for my current project, and make a few gentle strokes with the nib to get it flowing. I will also use these test strokes to determine if the ink is reacting properly with the paper or if there are issues that need to be addressed before continuing.

A word about writing with this type of pen: You will occasionally find that the ink doesn't want to flow on the paper. This can be caused by a blockage in the slit of the nib or you may be on a section of your page that has been exposed to oils from your hands. First and foremost, use a cover sheet of heavy Bristol paper to act as a guard between your grubby mitts and your pristine parchment. Secondly, don't try to use brute force to make it work, likely you will simply rip your paper or bend the tines of the nib. Think about writing as more coaxing the ink from the paper rather than forcing the ink to stick.

New nibs are commonly coated in a thin oil or wax which keeps them from rusting or otherwise discoloring while awaiting you to adopt them. This must be removed before use unless you enjoy fighting with ink blobs and inconsistent flow. I recommend using a bit of dish detergent in hot water. Soak the nibs for a few minutes then give them a bit of a scrub with a toothbrush. Rinse again in clean, warm water and dry with a lint-free cloth or chamois. There are some people who will advise you to heat your nib over a clean flame to burn off the waxes and oils. Avoid those kinds of people and kindly disregard their advice. You're more likely to destroy the integrity of the nib and clog it with soot than you are to clean it.

You should rinse your nibs in clean, warm water after use as well. I prefer to remove them from the nib holders and wipe dry after rinsing. In storage, I like to keep a silica-gel desiccant packet in their container to absorb any stray moisture in the air. Rust and chemical corrosion don't lend themselves to effective writing.

Heavily clogged nibs can be soaked in acetone or ammonia then brushed clean. Alternatively, an inexpensive ultrasonic jewelry cleaner can be utilized to power out the debris. Make certain to use an appropriate ultrasonic solution in your cleaner. Do I have to mention that you shouldn't mix random cleaning chemicals together? Just don't. Seriously.

As final word of caution, I must warn you; nibs tend to multiply in your collection over time. I'm unaware of the means by which they do it, I just know it happens. I started with a small variety package of five nibs and a holder. Today, they are taking over my toolbox. Even when I think I have corralled all the feral nibs into my toolbox, I still happen upon the occasional orphaned Speedball or a forlorn Brause. Consider yourself warned.

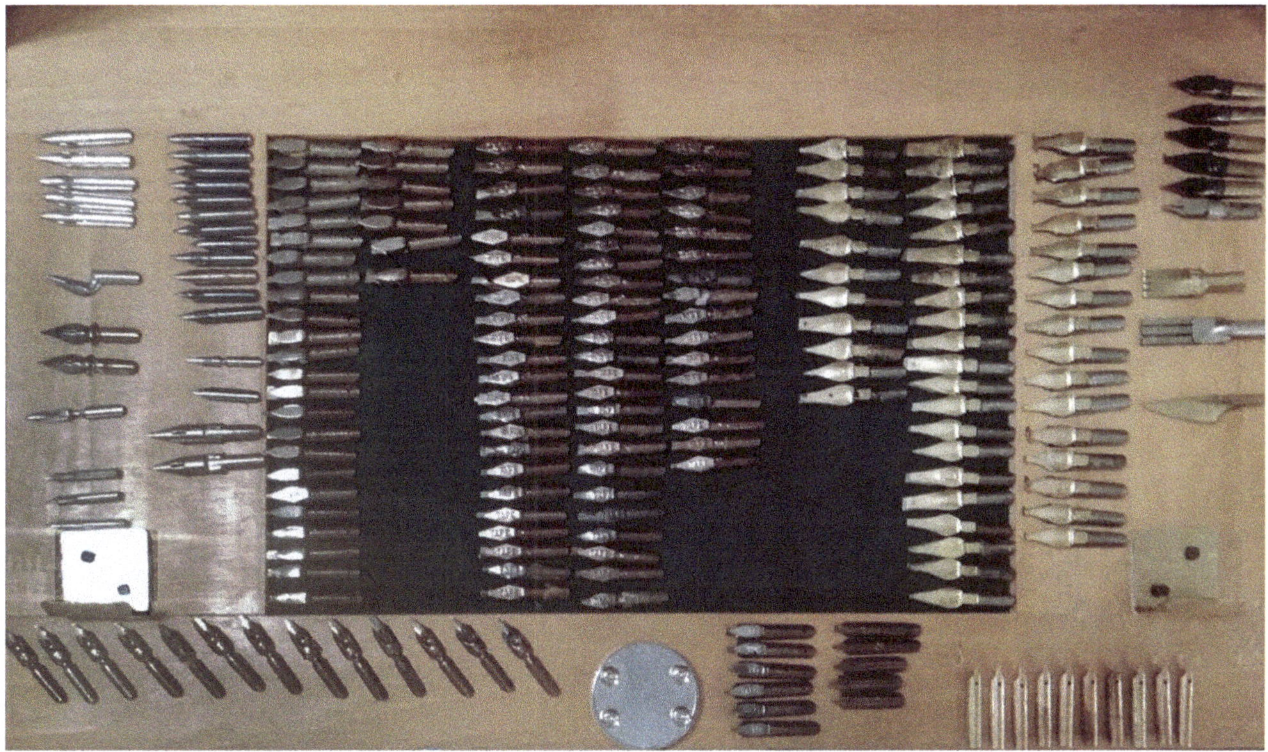

Figure 10 - A Fraction of the Author's Nib Hoard

Inks

*"Ink, dark as night, creates words, and as they are read,
they become the little beads and baubles of the mind."*

– Suzanne Valtsioti

There is something mystical about the relationship between pen, paper, and ink; The alchemy that catalyzes indelible marks to become vehicles of ideas and feelings. Throughout history, the human creature has found need of some substance with which to mark their presence in this world: ochre mixed with animal fats and applied to cave walls, soot and gums on papyrus, or modern polymers and dyes to print on bleached white paper. As calligraphers, it behooves us to have a basic understanding of the composition of ink and the differences between the types commonly available.

The composition of inks can vary greatly but they commonly involve a colorant and a vehicle or binder. The colorants can be either a pigment or a dye. Pigments are solid particulates in a suspension which provide color. Inks made with pigments tend to be more resistant to fading or bleaching. Dyes are aqueous solutions which can produce stronger colors but are also prone to bleeding and soaking through paper. The binders for both ink types can be water-soluble resins such as gum arabic, solvents, hide or fish glues, or some varnishes and oils.

Ink was invented in China and Egypt concurrently approximately 2600 BCE. Similar inks are still used today in India Ink. The Chinese imported bone black, lamp black, and other carbon sources from the Indian subcontinent, hence the nomenclature. Bone black is, as its name suggests, the ash resulting from the burning of animal bones. Lamp black is soot collected from the burning of tung oil and/or pine wood which had the resin stripped from it. Other sources of carbon black were basic charcoal made from vines or other vegetable matter. The Romans would later also use squid ink, sepia, for writing and drawing. They would have called this carbon-based ink *atramentum.*

Whatever the source of the carbon black, it would be finely ground, sifted, and separated resulting in a fine dust. This was then ground together with a mixture of hide or fish glue, water, and shellac (a resin secreted by the lac bug). The resulting ink could be stored in either liquid form or allowed to dry in rectangular molds. These would then be rubbed on ink stones with a few drops of water until the desired consistency is obtained.

Theophilus, in his 12th century work, described a decoction of Hawthorn wood, water, and wine to create a reddish-black ink. He also would describe a mixture of copperas (also known as vitriol or iron (II) sulfate) and oak galls to create an ink which, when applied to parchment, goes on blue-grey and quickly oxidizes to a rich black. The ink later fades to a nut-brown shade as can be seen in hundreds of medieval manuscripts; a testament to the popularity of the mixture. Pliny, roughly a thousand years prior to *On Divers Arts,* described vellum treated with copperas being marked with a tincture of nutgalls.

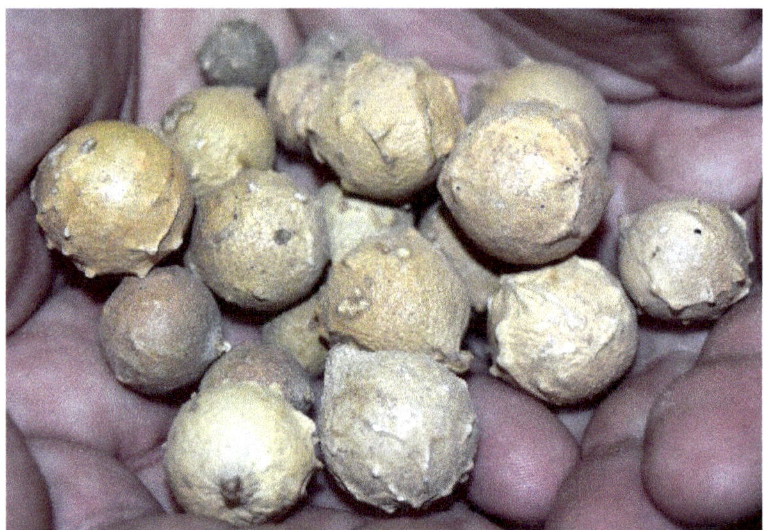

Figure 11 - Aleppo Oak Galls

PROJECT I: IRON-GALL INK

> **A Book Containing Divers Sorts of Hands**
> **by**
> **John de Beau Chesne and M. John Baildon**
> **Published in 1571.**
> "To make common yncke of Wyne take a quart,
> Two ounces of gomme, let that be a parte,
> Five ounces of galles, of copres take three,
> Long standing dooth make it better to be;
> If wyne ye do want, rayne water is best,
> And as much stuffe as above at the least:
> If yncke be to thick, put vinegar in,
> For water dooth make the colour more dimme.
> In hast for a shift when ye have a great nead,
> Take woll, or wollen to stand you in steede;
> which burnt in the fire the powder bette small
> With vinegre, or water make yncke with all.
> If yncke ye desire to keep long in store
> Put bay salte therein, and it will not hoare.
> Of that common yncke be not to your minde Some
> lampblack thereto with gomme water grinde"

If you are interested in trying your hand at making Iron-Gall ink, you will need to gather a few materials:

- 1.5 liters distilled water
- 1.0 liter white wine
- 85 grams Aleppo Oak Galls
- 14 grams Vitriol dissolved in 60 ml distilled water
- 14 grams Gum arabic dissolved in 60 ml distilled water

Between Amazon and John Neal Bookseller, you should be able to source the Vitriol (copperas, or Iron (II) Sulfate), and the Oak Galls. Don't worry, you won't end up on any government watchlists searching these out. I hope.

Begin by pulverizing the oak galls in a mortar and pestle until they are ¼"-minus. They don't need to be powdered, just crushed to increase the surface area. Bring the wine and water to a boil in a non-reactive vessel, add the galls and let simmer, covered, for at least 2 hours. You can strain the gall tea mixture and use it right away or let it stand for an additional 24 hours to fully extract the tannins from the oak galls then strain it.

When you are ready to proceed, I've found that warming the tea back up to blood temperature helps the next steps proceed smoothly. Using linen cloth or filter paper in a funnel, strain the tea then replace it into the pot you had used previously. Dissolve the vitriol completely in warm distilled water. Do the same with the gum arabic.

Now, make certain that you are not using one of your good cooking pots. Also, wear some clothes that you don't mind getting stained. Begin stirring the gall tea gently. Add the vitriol to the pot. The solution should turn black almost instantly. Add the gum arabic solution to thicken the ink. Finally, carefully decant the cool mixture into jars or tincture bottles with droppers.

Perhaps it's a bit late to mention that ink comes from a Greek word *enkaiein* meaning to 'burn in'. This ink will be somewhat acidic and can easily damage your steel nibs if you fail to clean them well after using it. A further bit of advice: if the ink is too thin, cautiously add a couple drops of the gum arabic solution from above. If it is too thick, you can always add a bit of white vinegar, wine, or distilled water to thin it out.

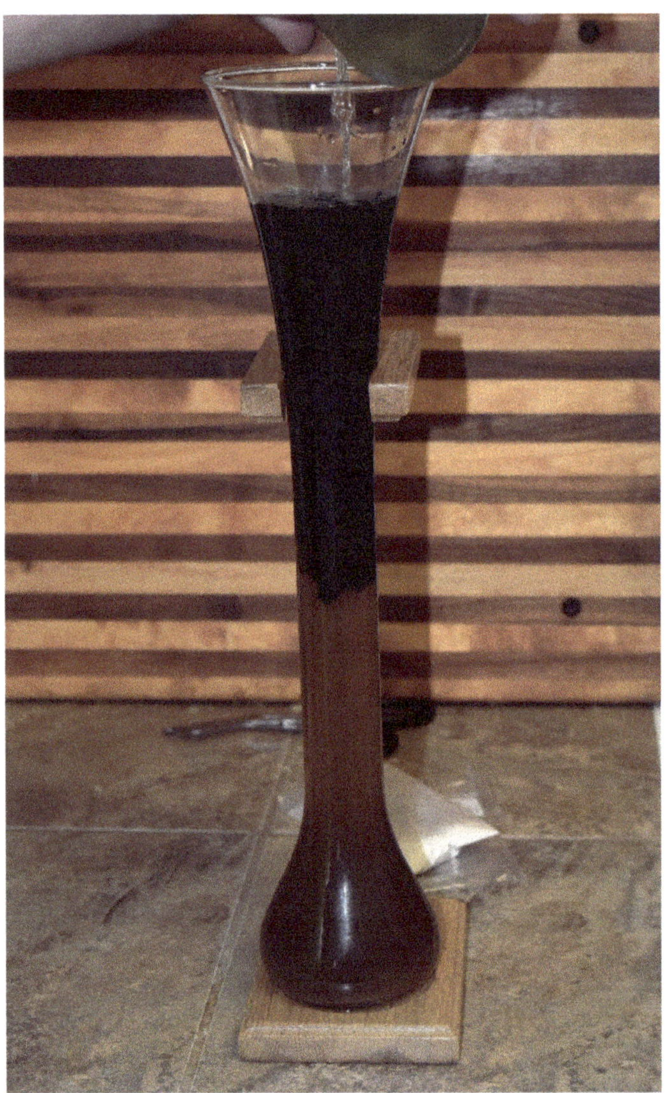

Figure 12 - A Half-Yard of Ink; Reaction of Copperas and Gallic Tea

Common Commercial Ink

If you are not up to making a mess of your kitchen, then perhaps I can interest you in some of the high quality, conveniently available inks for your use? The advantage of using commercially available inks is their consistency. Also, they tend to contain fewer ingredients which may be hazardous to your health. If you are using fountain or cartridge pens, the manufacturer of those pens will have suggested inks and cartridges specific to their pens. Deviating from their suggestions can lead to a permanently clogged pen, damaged nib, or just poor performance overall.

For your dip pens, I'm a fan of either Higgins Eternal or Black Magic. Eternal is a permanent, non-waterproof, carbon based black ink whereas Black Magic is waterproof. I have used Higgins Eternal safely in many fountain pens and cartridge pens with the piston refill cartridge. The dropper in the Black Magic bottle is the absolute perfect size for reloading 99% of my nibs. Both inks also provide excellent coverage, flow smoothly, and dry rapidly without bleeding.

Ideally you will want an ink that is lightfast (not prone to discolor or fade on exposure to light), permanent, and pH neutral. There are scads of different inks, of all colors, on the market. Take your time, try what you find, and stick with what works the best for you. Don't forget that one ink will work differently with different nibs, different brands of nibs, and even within specific size ranges. The key is to simply experiment and keep meticulous notes about what you prefer.

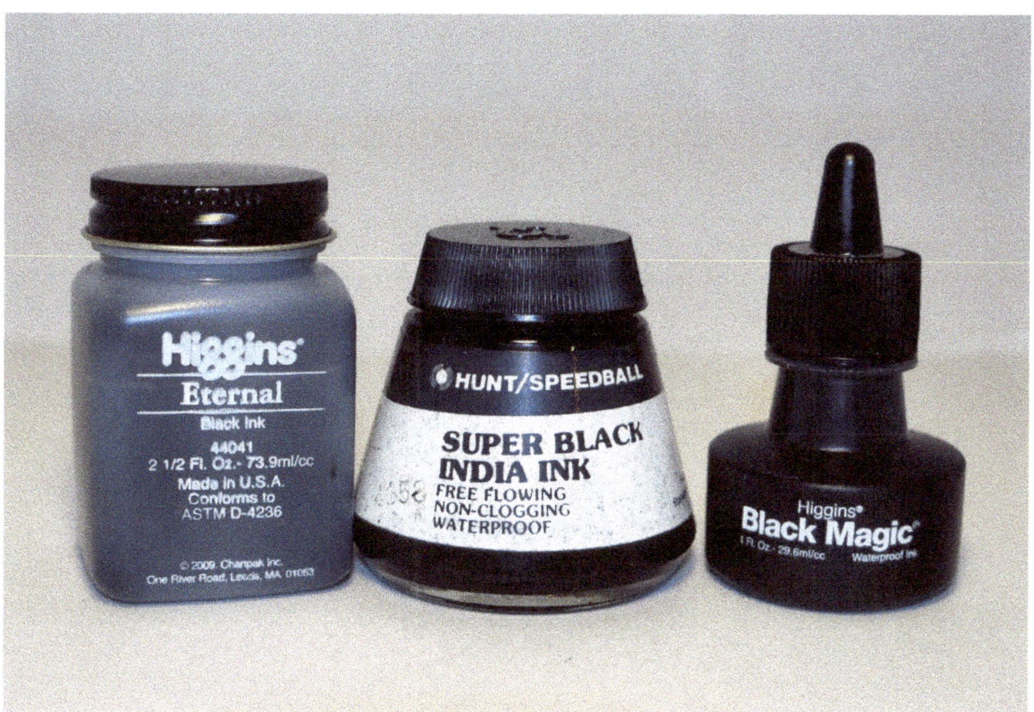

Figure 13 - A Trio of Commercially Available Inks

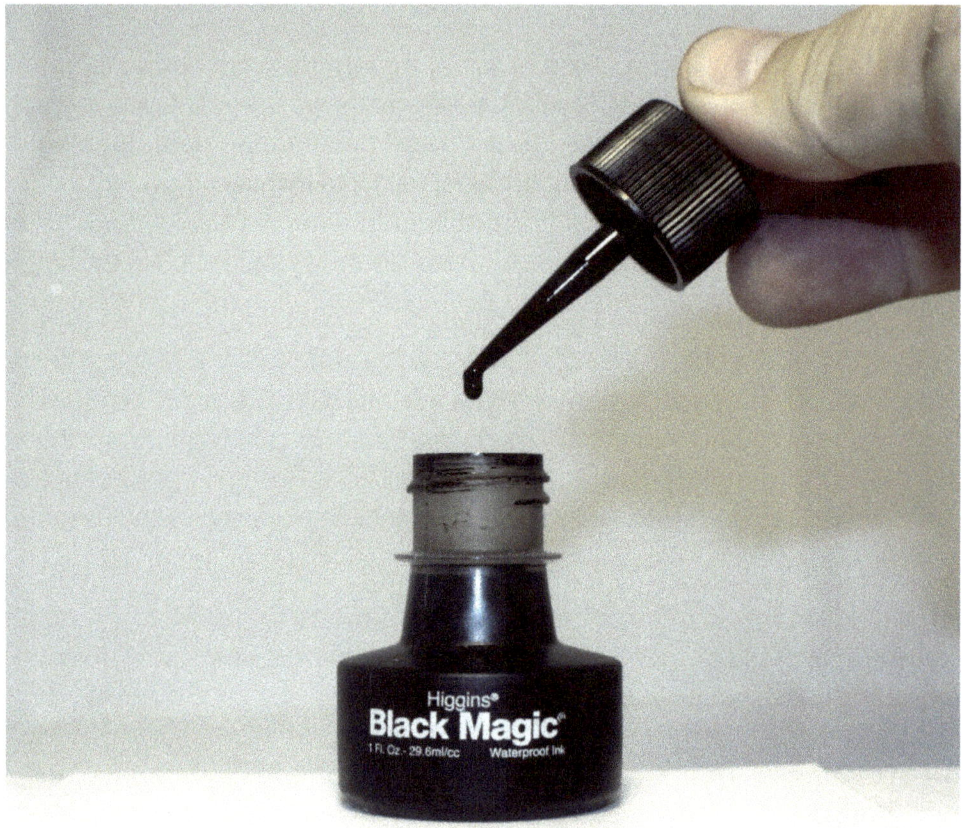

Figure 14 - It's Hard Not to Love Black Magic

Paper

The paper that we are all familiar with has a surprisingly long history. Paper, in this case, being plant or cloth fibers pounded to a pulp then felted on a fine mesh or screen, pressed, and dried. Wood-pulp paper didn't come on the scene until the 19th century CE.

The earliest known extant fragment of paper was unearthed at Fangmatan, an archaeological site located near Tianshui, China. It is dated to around 179 BCE. The earliest paper document known in Europe is the *Mazarab Missal of Silos*, currently held in the library of the Monastery of Santo Domingo de Silos in Spain. It dates to the late 11th century CE, possibly earlier.

In order to be made usable for pen and ink, paper requires a substance called sizing to be applied to its surface. The sizing smooths the surface of the paper, giving it a texture amenable for a pen to move across, and preventing ink from blotting and running through the fibers. Early papers where sized with wheat or rice starch which left them susceptible to rotting. Later, animal-based glues were used as sizing which increased the lifespan and durability of the pages. Modern papers are sized using a bewildering hodgepodge of chemicals, optical brighteners, and other unspeakable trade secrets.

Bristol board or Bristol paper is frequently used by calligraphers as well as illustrators, cartoonists, and the occasional draughtsperson. It is an uncoated, layered stock which is generally found in white but can be purchased in other colors and is around 220 to

250 g/m². Bristol's surface is either plate (also called smooth) or vellum finish. Plate finish is ideal for our purposes and is characterized by a platen like surface. The vellum finish is better for charcoal, pastels, and the like as it is more textured.

Pergamenata is another very common paper used by reenactors. It has the look and feel of animal parchment, it's highly sized, and takes ink very well. It comes in grammages of 160 and 230 g/m². It is made by the Fredrigoni company and comes in natural or antique colors. I recommend using the heavyweight variety if you will be adding illumination to your project, it resists curling and warping better than the 160 gsm weight. Fabriano's version of this paper is called Pergamon and is similar in nearly every way.

Watercolor paper is another terrific option for calligraphy and illumination. Minimum standards for the majority of work are 140 lb./300 gsm, hot press, satin finish. Arches Watercolor Blocks, I have found, are ideal. A block of 300 gsm from Arches consists of 20 sheets of gelatin-sized, pH neutral, acid free paper that are bound on all four sides. These sheets can take heavy watercolor washes and thick applications of gouache and gilding without buckling.

Vellum and Parchment

Sadly, the terms 'vellum' and 'parchment' have become so confounded over the years that entire books have been written simply trying to define them. Parchment, originally, referred to any animal skin that has been treated for the purpose of writing. Vellum, specifically, was calfskin parchment. Parchment now seems to refer to anything vaguely antique looking and made from animal, vegetable, or plastic; but I digress.

Animal parchments can be found prepared either one-sided or double-sided. The double-sided sheets are called manuscript preparations. Single-sided tend to have the hair side ready to write on. If you're confused by all of this, don't worry. It will become much clearer over time and through more study.

Whatever type of animal parchment you decide to use, it will need to be prepared before use. The surface will need to be sanded to a delicate tooth using fine dental pumice. Brushed clean, any excess oils will need to be handled using a pounce – finely ground gum sandarac in a linen bag. Keep the pounce nearby, if you run into any portion of a sheet wherein the ink doesn't want to take or it tries to run, apply the pounce. Don't forget to brush off any extra sandarac with a clean, soft brush.

Due to the non-absorbent nature of parchment, I find iron-gall ink to work the best. Iron-gall 'bites' into the surface and creates a permanent mark over time. If a mistake is made, and caught early enough, one can scrape the dry ink off the skin, burnish the surface with a piece of polished agate, and pounce the area before re-writing the correct word or letter. Oh yeah, mistakes happen, just blame it on Titivillus, the Patron Demon of Scribes.

Writing Slope

A writing slope is simply an inclined surface on which you are able to work comfortably. Whether you use a purpose-made writing desk circa 12th century CE, or a hunk of sanded and varnished plywood propped up on books, having a large surface angled at 45° to 60° from horizontal is essential to good form and comfortable practice.

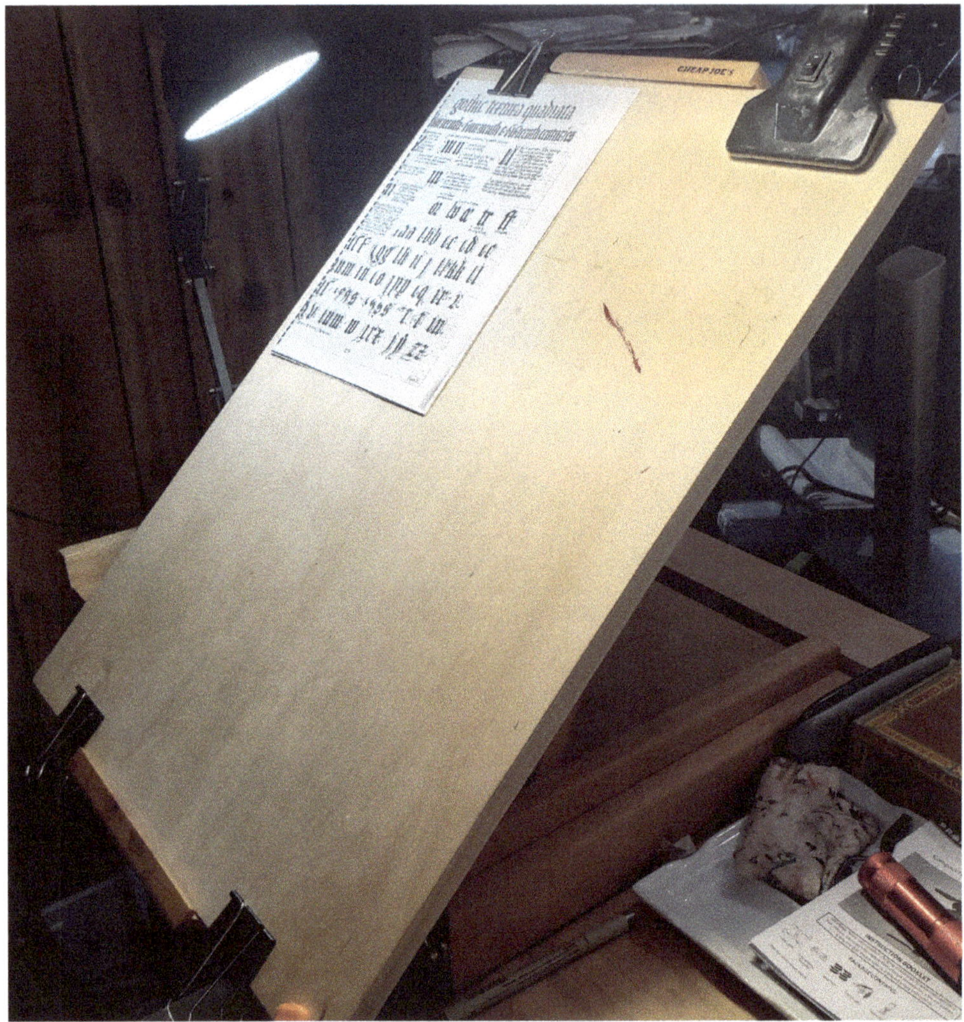

Figure 15 - The Author's Writing Slope

I frequently use a commercially available drawing board on a portable easel/paintbox as shown in Figure 15. Please note the large binder clips and the multiple light sources.

II. HOW TO PRACTICE

Practice is a word that many of us dislike hearing. It is a process that involves repetition, trial and error, and frequent failure. It is the frequent failure bit that tends to turn many people from calligraphy.

Here's a bit of a reality check: calligraphy is difficult. More accurately, it is difficult to do well and consistently. Let's think about it for a moment though. As children learning to write our ABCs in grammar school, we were hardly masters of penmanship at the very beginning; not even close. We were learning how to make strange marks with strange tools and being scolded for exhibiting this vague condition called "poor penmanship". I had a teacher in fifth grade who would smack our knuckles with the small edge of a wooden yardstick for turning in an assignment with "poor penmanship". Not an effective method of teaching, in my opinion.

As adults or possibly adolescents interested in learning this art, you stand at the precipice once again. Sure, now you know your alphabet a little better, but we are still making strange marks with strange tools! My chief advice to you, should you choose to go forward on this adventure, is simply to relax. Beyond that: practice!

Practice frequently and rest frequently. Several shorter sessions will do more for you than one long marathon session done rarely. Find ways to use calligraphy in your daily life to give you dozens of mini-practice sessions every day. Writing a check? Callig that bank-draft! Birthday card? Make it extra special with a bit of calligraphic flair. Grocery lists, love notes, ex libris in your books: all are very effective ways to practice your art and spread beautiful lettering as you go.

A few more things to consider as you begin to practice: Start by using calligraphy markers. That's right, use those multi-colored, chisel-edge, felt-tip, cheap markers! Using dip or fountain pens adds an additional layer of complexity to the process of learning how to write (again). So, don't make it doubly difficult for yourself: grab a marker and work on your lettering. You can always go back later and learn to use the other flavors of pens. For now, let's keep it simple.

Pick a single calligraphic hand to practice until you can perform it consistently. Only then should you move on to the next hand on your hit list. If you are like most people, you want to do all the hands right away! Settle down, you'll get there. It is just going to take a bit of time and, wait for it...practice!

I am aware that a lot of novices want to learn Gothic Textura Quadrata or something equally showy first. I feel comfortable in saying that you will progress faster, achieve more satisfaction, and build a more solid foundation of pen skills if you start with Carolingian Miniscule. Then, after having reached a degree of proficiency and consistency in that hand, move on to another.

My reasoning is this: the work that you do with Carolingian will develop the muscle control and attention to detail necessary to not get absolutely frustrated with the precision that Gothic and other hands require. Moreover, Carolingian is similar to what we are accustomed to seeing every day in modern fonts and in the (printed) handwriting which we're taught in school. Therefore, the transition into calligraphy is simplified. This is only a suggestion, but I have seen students in my classes do better overall and stay with calligraphy longer when they started with Carolingian rather than one of the blackletter/gothic hands.

If possible, take in-person, hands-on classes from an experienced and reputable teacher. Seeing someone else's techniques for writing in calligraphy, workspace layout, etc. will only serve to help build your own skills and confidence. Also, a good teacher will be able to spot possible problems with your own technique and help you avoid pitfalls that are inherent in self-education.

III. POSTURE AND BODY MECHANICS

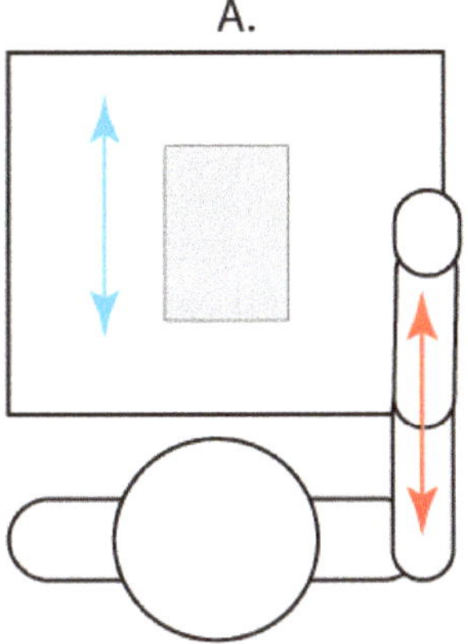
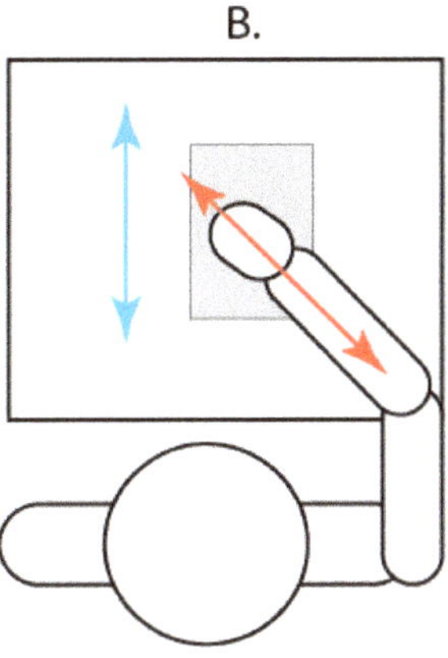
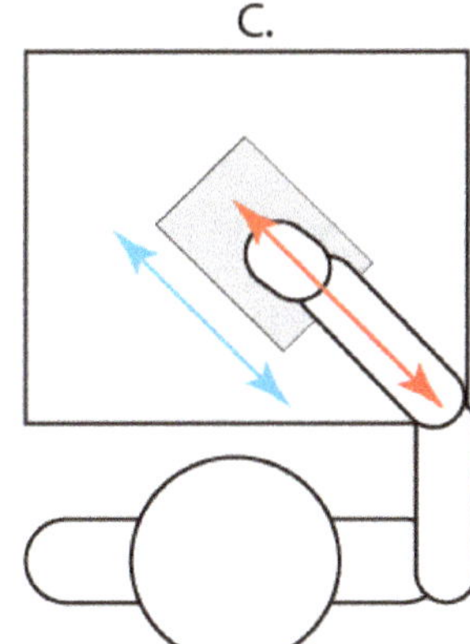

Figure 16 - Angle of Writing

It may surprise you to discover that your body doesn't like moving in straight lines, at least not directly. The combination of fingers, wrist, forearm, upper arm, and shoulder provide the human form a myriad of unique abilities if they can all learn to work together as a single unit. If we add in the need to see what we are doing, then things get a bit more complicated.

Figure 16-A illustrates the problem of the angles of writing. In order to view the page on which we are writing, without distortion, we need it to be in the center of our visual field. To draw a straight line without our elbow intersecting with our ribcage requires clearance around and away from the body. In this situation, not much writing is going to take place.

Bringing the arm into the center of the writing slope and at a natural, comfortable angle increases the motion around and away from the body (Figure 15-B). The upper arm is still driving the motion, but it is from a less constrictive movement. This is all well and good, but the orientation of the paper leaves much to be desired: few calligraphic hands feature a backwards slant.

This may have been a long way to go to explain something that most of us had been taught in elementary school penmanship. However, I feel it is important to know why we do certain things the way we do them. We tend to forget these little details over time, and it costs us dearly. Figure 16-C shows a page rotated to match what I call the 'natural straight-line movement' of the arm. It may take a bit of trial and error to find the exact angle, but you will find it over time. This is the angle and the posture that allows you to draw perfectly vertical lines parallel to the vertical edges of the paper.

Working on a slanted writing slope will likely take some getting used to as well. Start with an inclination of 30° and gradually increase the angle over time to between 45° and 60°. Yes, you can do calligraphy without the slope, it simply isn't ideal. Being hunched over a horizontal surface, as we know from school, is not conducive to comfortable, beautiful writing. An inclined writing slope opens the diaphragm, thus easing our respirations, and removes stress to the upper gastro-intestinal tract. A comfortable scribe is a happy scribe!

Sit up straight, drop your shoulders, and for goodness' sake, relax your jaw! Relax your fingers too. You do not have to strangle the pen to get it to write well. After it inexplicably leaves its sixth consecutive ink splotch on that expensive, creamy vellum then you are well justified in strangling the pen. Until then, just hold it firmly but gently.

Take frequent breaks as you practice. You will do better without the muscle cramps that come with marathon practice sessions. Your frustration levels will also be kept much lower in taking much needed intermissions.

Finally, learn to breathe more consciously. The act of breathing causes your body to move. A transient move on a tiny, delicate letter may incorporate an unsightly error that you will have to repair. Slow, deep breaths as you write can turn your scribal practice into a meditation. Take a slow deep breath, hold it a moment as you place the nib in position, and slowly exhale with the stroke.

Focus only on the task at hand. In the practice of calligraphy, allow me to quote Baba Ram Dass, "Be Here Now." (Dass, 1978) Be part of what you are writing. Put part of you into all that you do.

IV. GETTING STARTED

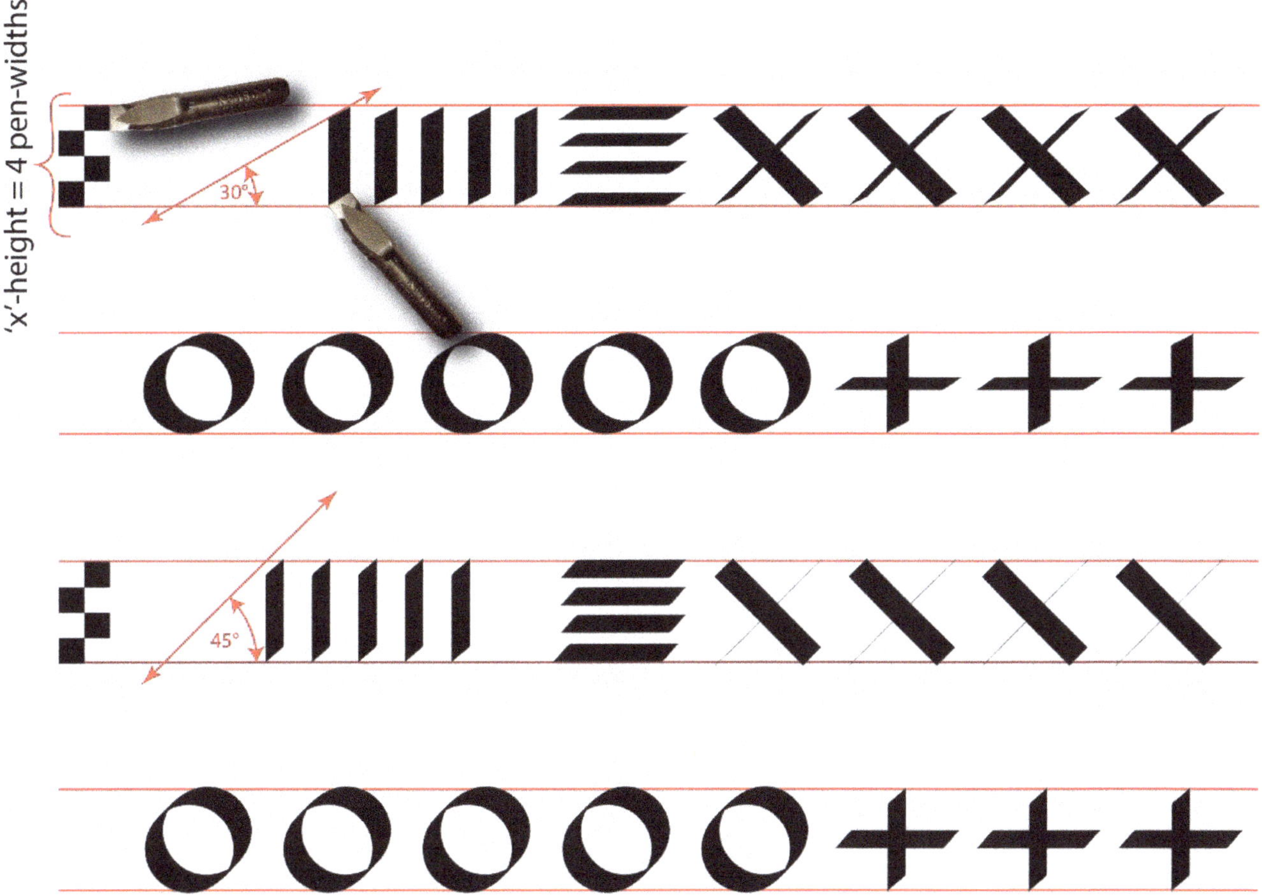

Figure 17 - Practice Strokes and Pen Angles

You're ready to get started, aren't you? You have assembled a small kit of tools and are just itching to play with them. Well, let's get on with it then!

For these exercises, you will need a pencil (I prefer a 0.3 mm mechanical pencil with 2H or 4H graphite but a basic wooden #2 sharpened nicely will work just fine), a ruler, a large chisel-tip calligraphy marker or pen, and several sheets of paper.

Measure down from the top of the page about 2-inches and draw a light, horizontal line using your pencil; this is your baseline. Next, using your calligraphy marker, make a stack of pen-width squares 4 or 5 pen-widths tall on the baseline. Draw another horizontal pencil line, parallel to the baseline, on top of the stack of squares. These two lines define the 'x'-height or the minim.

With your marker in hand, match the 30° angle seen in the figure and draw five vertical lines then stop. Put the pen down. Looking at your lines, ask yourself: "Are they straight or curvy? Are they vertical or do they lean to one side or the other?" Make five more vertical lines and reassess your work. Keep going until you are consistently making straight, clean, vertical lines then move on to the next stroke exercise.

As a side note/rant, be honest with yourself but be nice. Don't say, "This looks like crap, I'm never going to get this." Instead, use more positive self-talk, "This looks ok, but I know I can do better." While this may sound like some new age neuro-linguistic programming or some other psychology fad, it is a proven fact that positive self-talk is as helpful to the learning process as negative self-talk is detrimental. If you tell yourself you are going to be bad at something, you're right; you will be.

I know that these exercises can get boring quickly. However, just like stretching before exercising, they are warm-ups for the mind and body to get ready to perform. When you are preparing to do longer and more involved calligraphic works, the warm-up exercises become much more important. For now, of course, they're part of your learning process: you are training your fingers, hand, arm, body, eyes, and mind to work in concert to execute a complex set of movements. You're also learning how this silly flat-edged pen is supposed to work. Take your time and do your best. It will benefit you greatly in the future.

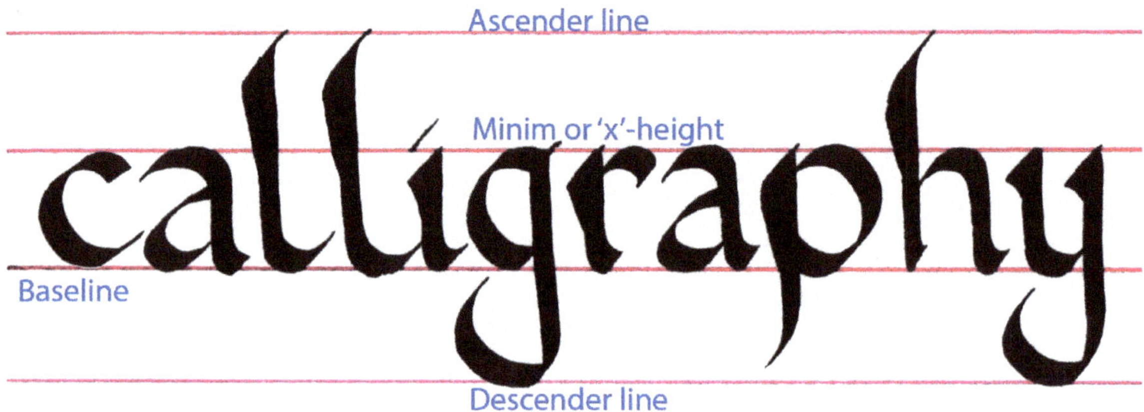

Figure 18 - Various Lines of Calligraphy

V. CALLIGRAPHIC HANDS AND INTERPRETATION

Before we begin looking at, and practicing, the individual calligraphic hands, it behooves me to mention that there are truly no master templates for any of these hands. Surely you can point to several characteristics during a specified time period and state, "because of features x, y, and z, this is an example of Insular Majuscule," and you would likely be both correct and incorrect! In paleographic discussions, there will always be somebody willing to point out that "this particular hand is more appropriately identified as…" Ignore them. For now, at least, ignore them.

Even within the same monastery at the same period there are vast differences between the commonly used hand. In fact, within individual manuscripts there can be variations in the lettering performed by the same scribe. The reality is that letter forms are as individual as the people creating them. As you start out, follow the given forms. Later, with study, research, and exposure to more manuscript images and examples from other calligraphers, you can comfortably add your own personalized touches to the hands you're using.

If you are creating a piece that is inspired by a specific manuscript, then spend the time browsing images of the manuscript pages. Create a catalog of the letters as you go through it. Note any variations between letters found at the beginning or in the middle of a word as opposed to at the end of a word or a line. Once you have an idea for the feel and character of the individual letters you will be well equipped to create your interpretation of that script.

Even as you browse current literature and textbooks you will find a considerable amount of variation between classic calligraphic hands. Your Speedball Textbook might disagree with Drogin, and your Drogin may disagree with…well…you get the idea. In the end, these are all interpretations and wild generalizations. Simply focus on beautiful writing for now and sweat the technical details later. Oh, and don't forget to have fun!

PROJECT 2: IN THE BEGINNING...

Before we start, I would like you to find a box large enough to hold your practice sheets but not so large that it will be awkward to use. Shoeboxes for hiking boots are perfect for this but your local craft store would likely have any number of similar items that would work. It simply needs to be able to hold what you have done and keep it safe.

Every time you fill a sheet of practice paper with calligraphy, every time you doodle a letter, everything...I want you to put the date on it and save it in this box. As you progress over the next month, six-months, a year, take the box out and revisit where you started and compare it with where you are at that moment. You will definitely see improvement!

When you are having a rough time with your practice, the items in this box are reminders that you are getting better. They are a concrete example of your hard work and dedication. Moreover, they are a journal of your progress which you can use to identify and fix any problem areas you may have in your calligraphy.

Bonus points: decorate your box! Have some fun and be a kid again. This also helps start activating the creative side of your brain – it's in for a workout.

VI. THE UNCIAL MAJUSCULE HAND

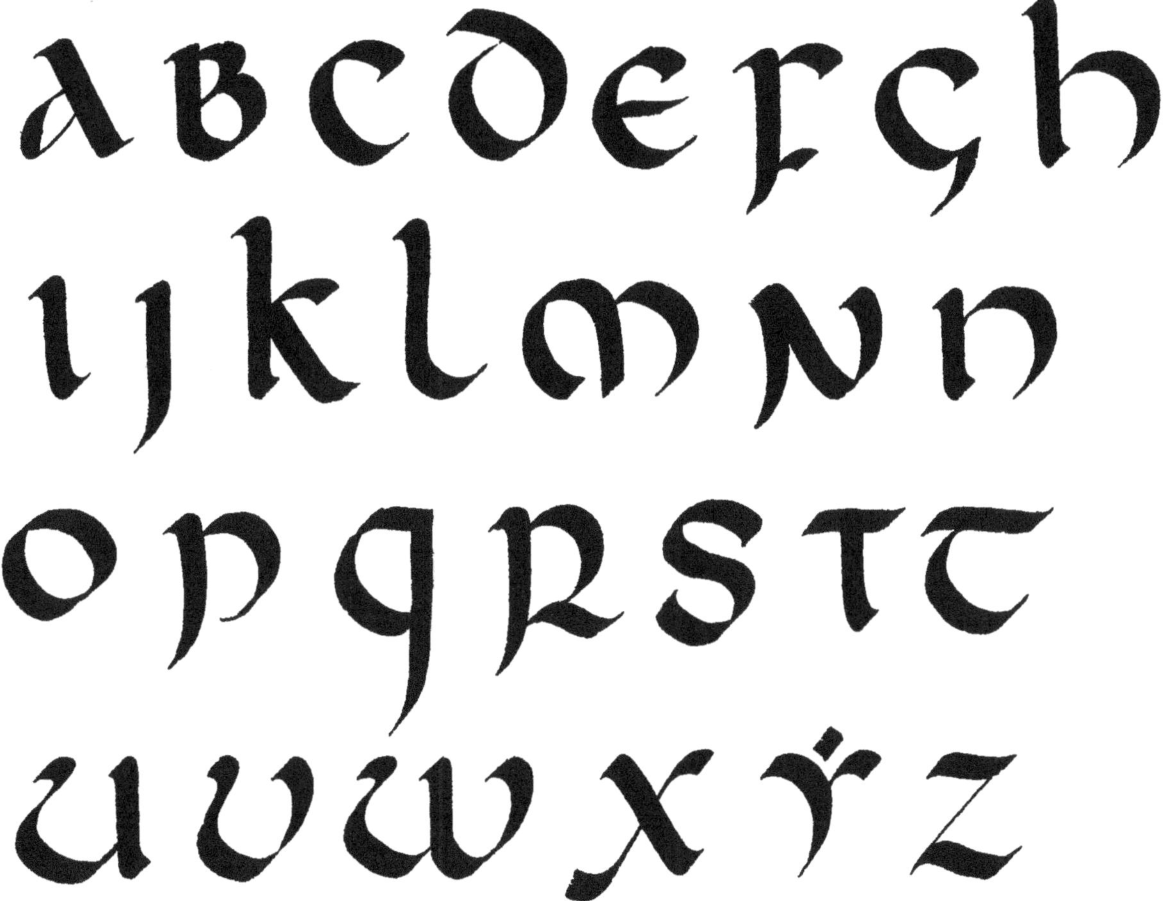

Figure 19 - Uncial Majuscule Exemplar

Uncial is a family of majuscule scripts used throughout the world from 300 CE to 900 CE predominantly by Latin and Greek scribes. The term majuscule refers to the script being written in all capitals. It likely evolved from a much earlier form of Rustic Roman. It should be remembered that these dates are only general guidelines as forms of Uncial can be observed as early as the 1st century and their use carried over as versals even into the late Middle Ages and the Renaissance.

One of the defining characteristics of Uncial is the simple, rounded forms with a serif constructed using a slight twist of the pen. The letters are penned with a letter height of 4 to 5 pen widths and a pen angle of approximately 30° from the baseline. Vertical strokes should show a slight arc instead of rigid verticality.

Uncial Ductus

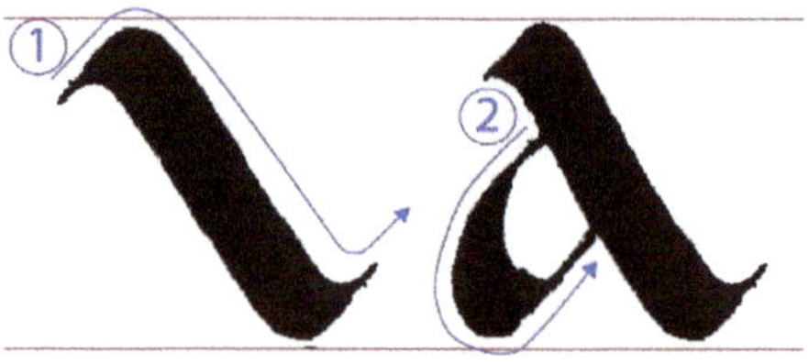

The x-height of the letters in this ductus (the strokes that make up a written letter) is 4 nib-widths and the letters are penned at 30°. The A is composed of two strokes. In the first stroke. The pen slides upward diagonally left to right to create a hairline serif (decorative projection found in a stroke of a letter) before descending diagonally down to the baseline. A gentle flick of the pen at the bottom of the stroke will add a nice final serif as well. The second stroke begins approximately 2/3 of the way up the first stroke, creating a gentle curve to the baseline. The left-hand corner of the pen is used to sweep upwards in a thin line at about 1/3 the way up the first stroke.

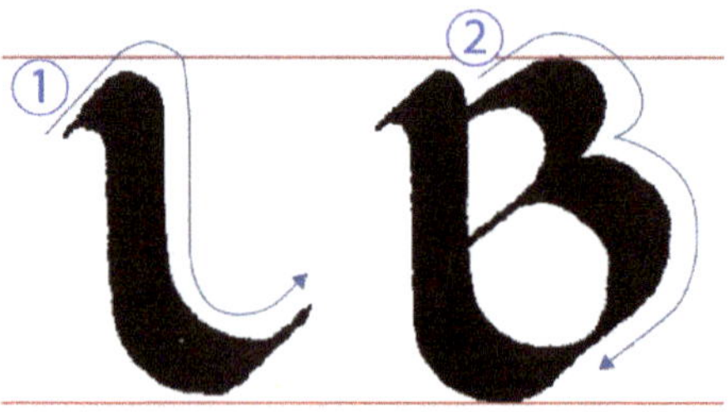

The B starts with the hairline slide from left to right, vertically descending until a soft curve is formed for the base of the B starting at about 1/3 of the overall height from the baseline then sweeping up. The second stroke does a little curvaceous bump-bump before meeting the terminal end of the initial stroke in a thin hairline union. Be careful to maintain your hairlines as thin as possible, especially where strokes one and two meet.

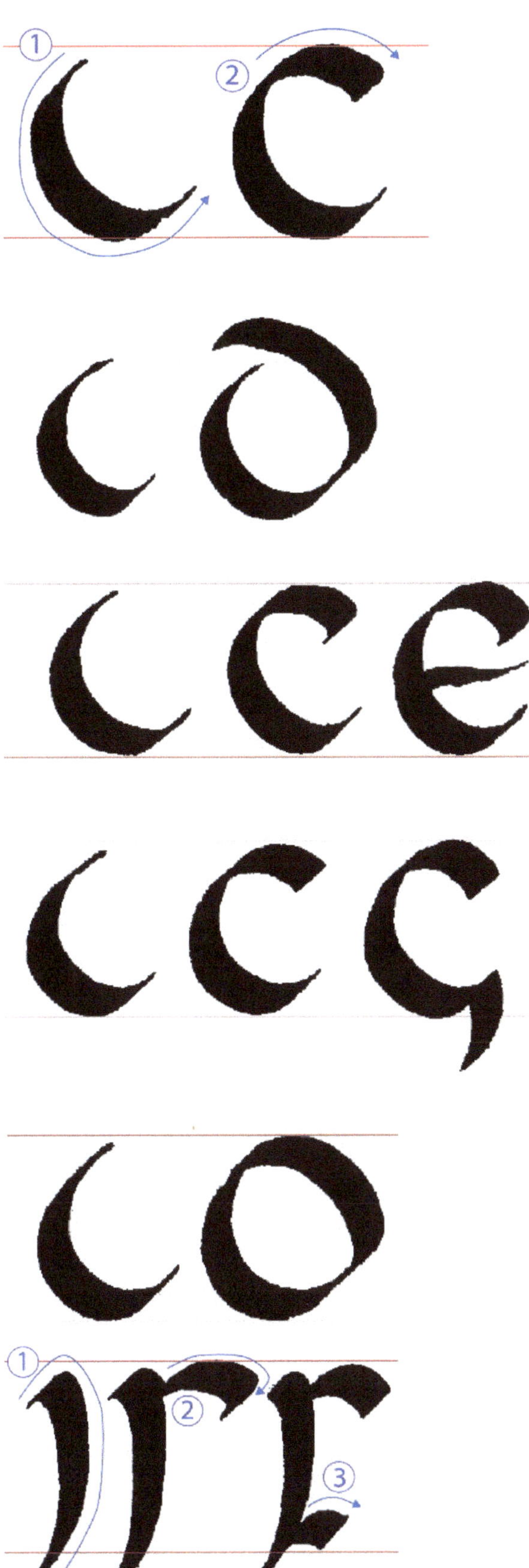

C, as well as D, E, G, and O follow much the same pattern. Uncial's characteristic rounded letters are penned with a sweeping circular arc, beginning and ending with thin lines. For the second stroke on these letters, a rounded cap on the E and G ends with a slight flick of the pen for a serif. The O would finish connecting with the end of the first stroke. The D has a similar cap, it just is elevated and ends similarly to the O. The G is identical to the C but is sticking its tongue out at the letters beneath it!

Do I have to mention the slide into the main stroke or the decorative flick anymore? It's here on the F as well. Some variations on Uncial have straight vertical strokes in a number of letters. I prefer a little bit of an arc as can be seen in a number of manuscripts. With the F, try to keep it from looking as if it is falling on its face!

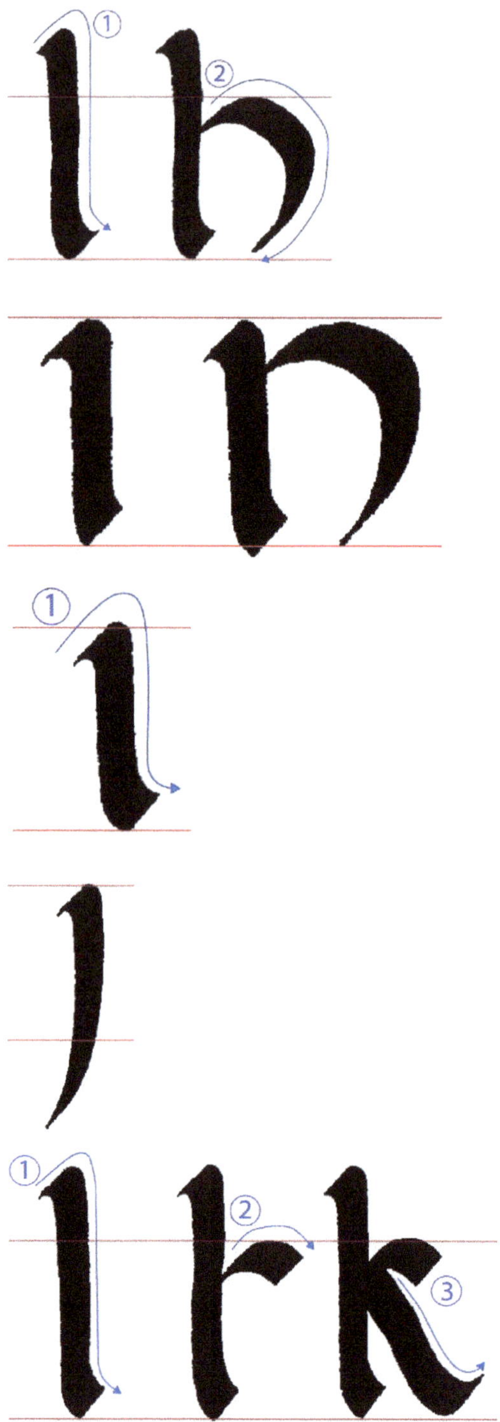

The H and the N are very similar in form; N having an x-height vertical stroke and the H reaching into ascender space. There are some variations wherein a small 'foot' serif is added, but that is a personal touch I will leave you to decide for yourself. Otherwise, keep an eye on the roundness of the second stroke on each of these letters. It is easy to flatten it accidentally, giving it a punched-in appearance.

The I is deceptively simple. Be sure to keep it vertical. You may add a small tittle (the small stroke or dot seen over the modern I) or leave it off entirely.

The J, in contrast, has a slight arc to it and ends below the baseline in a fine point. The addition of a tittle is again up to you. If you do add the stroke, however, I recommend adding it to the I as well to maintain consistency.

The K has the straight ascender like the H, keep it vertical and without any arc. Keep a smooth arc on the second stroke, allowing enough room for your pen to come back in for the final stroke. If any letter deserves a bit of careful attention, the K will certainly benefit from extra practice. Your work and patience will surely be rewarded.

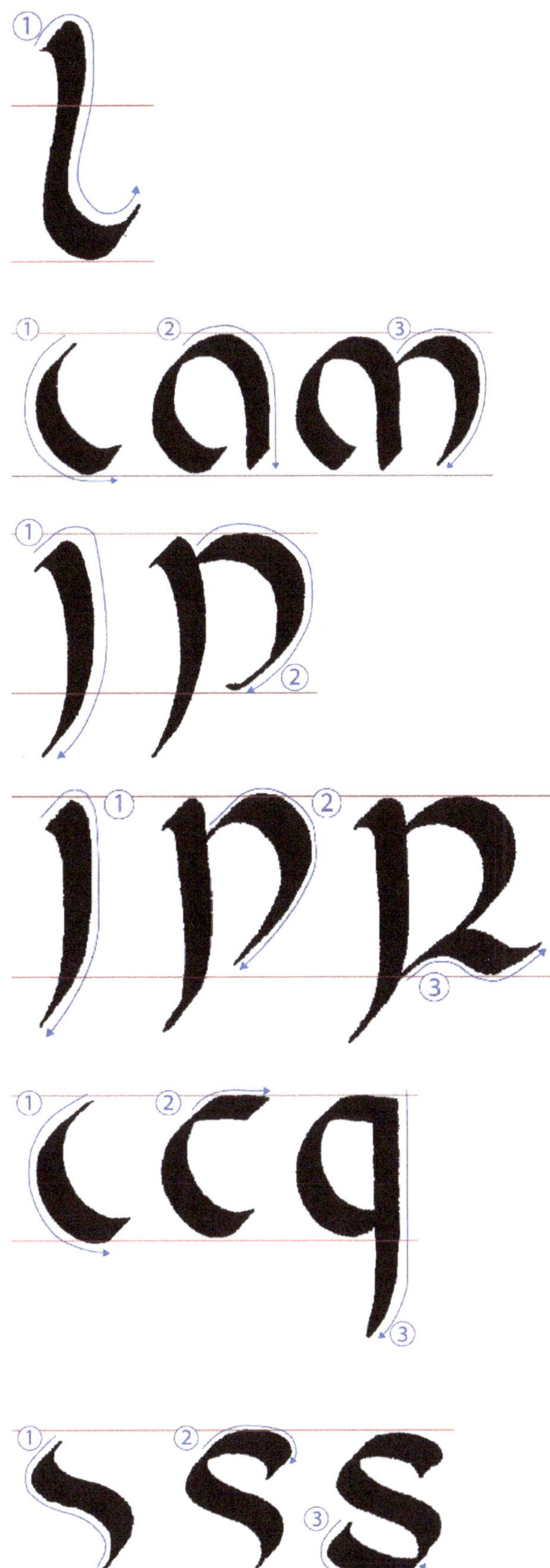

L is a very curvaceous letter! A gentle sweeping arc gradually transitioning into a rounded bottom that rests neatly on the baseline highlights this variation. As simple as it may seem, getting the combination of curves to work together in a single stroke can take some effort. Never fear, it will all come together with practice.

Speaking of curvy letters, the M can be a bit of a tricky one to master. In this case, keeping a balance between the left-hand and the right-hand curves takes a little practice. Take a breath between each stroke, don't race through its formation.

The P features the arcing vertical stroke that dips below the baseline. On the second stroke, make sure to keep it round. It is perfectly acceptable to not close that bottom gap, I promise. Just keep the end of the stroke thin.

The R is formed much like the P only with the addition of a wiggly tongue jutting out in front. Visually, I prefer a slightly straighter vertical stroke rather than the arced version. This is simply my personal preference, of course, and you are free to exercise your creative freedom.

The Q should be round on the left-hand side and vertical until the very last moment on the right-hand descender. You can use the slightly straighter cap as shown in stroke 2 or you can have some fun and introduce a slight downward curve where it meets the descender. Both versions were seen commonly in Uncial manuscripts, occasionally even within the same manuscript!

S needs practice to make it look balanced and to keep it from appearing as if it were in rotation. Take your time and focus on establishing an even set of curves in the first stroke. The cap in stroke 2 should just graze

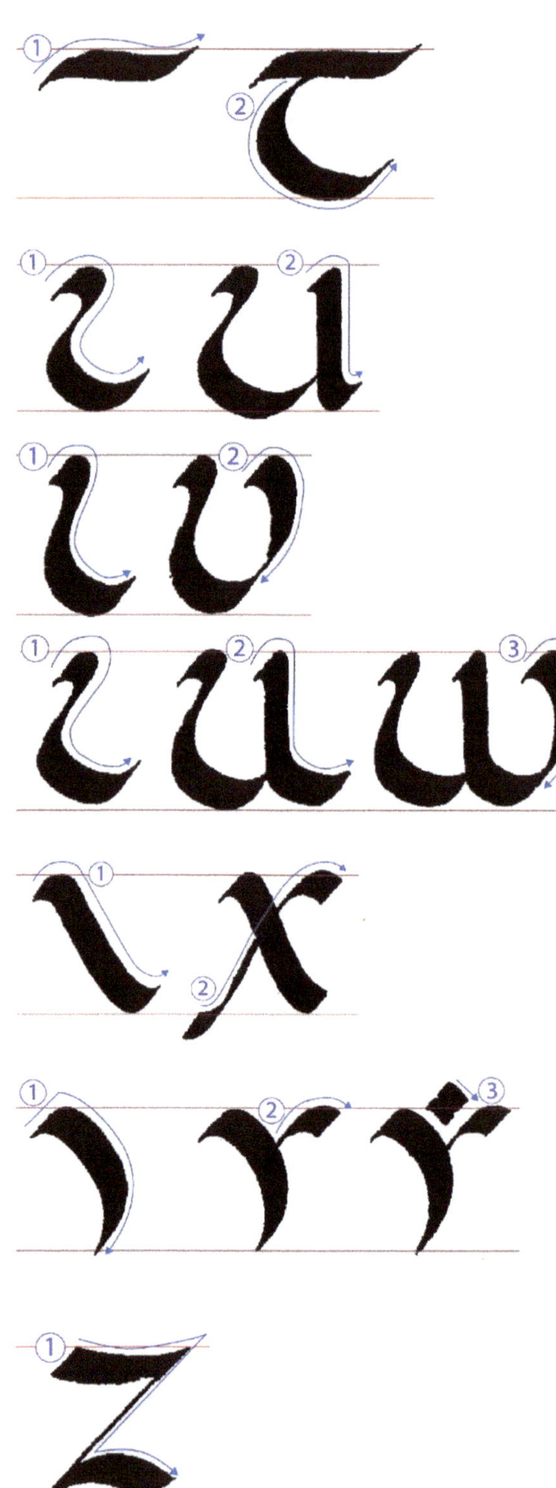

the upper guideline before curving downwards. Stroke 3 should neatly tie into the end of stroke 1.

The T is relatively straightforward. One mistake I see many beginners make frequently is in reversing the order of the strokes. In doing so, the thin joint portion of the letter tends to get lost, ending in a very clunky looking letter.

U, V, and W are incredibly similar. Keep them balanced and work on graceful, round curves for the bodies of the letters. There are a number of variations on how to start the initial 'hook' or serif on the first strokes, so find one that is comfortable for you.

The real trick to creating the X is in mastering the upwards sweeping second stroke without leaving a splotch of ink when your pen inevitably hits a phantom speed bump on your paper. Otherwise, it too is rather straightforward.

Yes, that is a dotted Y. Why? That's just the way it was done. Frankly, I like it! Curve that first stroke down and back; you can even let it dip a pen width or two below the baseline. As for the dot, make it a nice diamond shape and keep it well centered in the gap between the first two strokes.

Z is best done in a single stroke. Watch the curves on the top and bottom. The center diagonal stroke is to be as straight as you can make it and thin.

VII. CAROLINGIAN

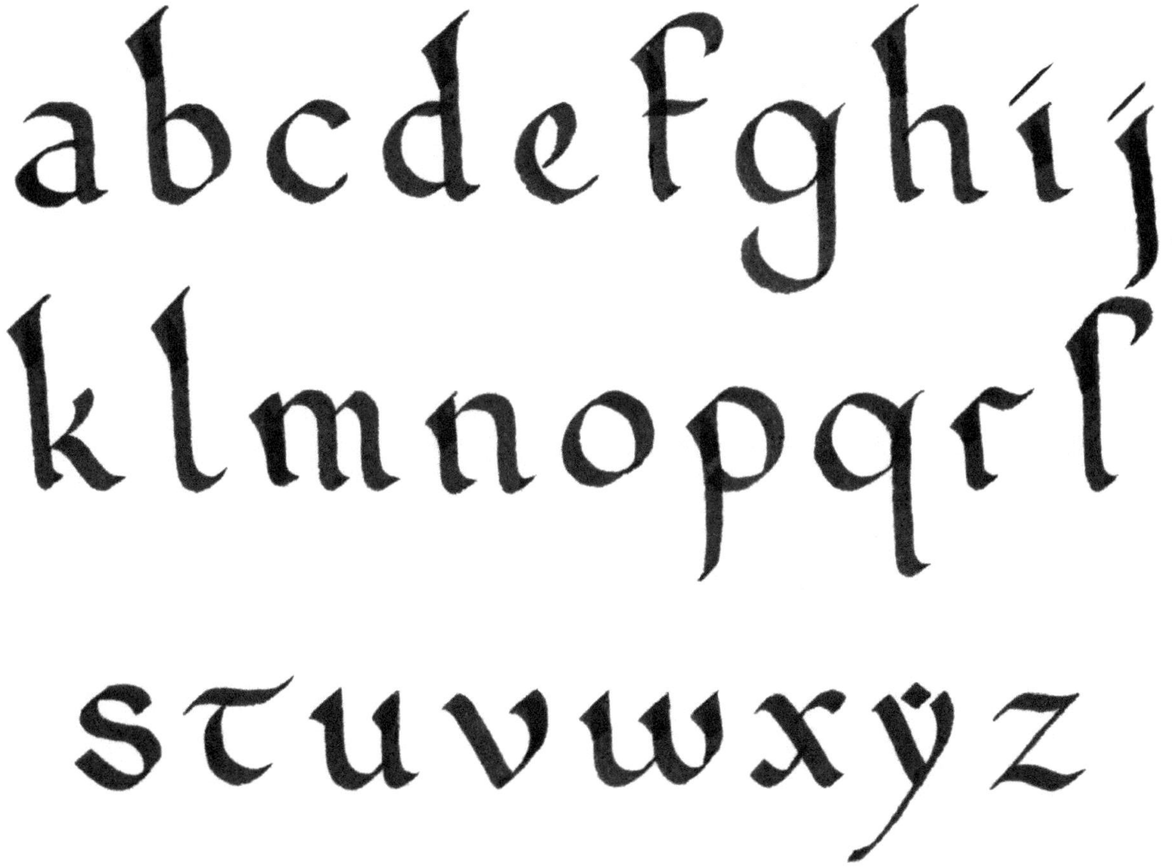

Figure 20 - Carolingian Miniscule Exemplar

Carolingian Miniscule (or minuscule, there's quite a bit of contention concerning the spelling of that one) was used from the 700s to the 1100s CE. Under Charlemagne's patronage, the Benedictine monk Alcuin of York developed this easily recognized script for wide use throughout the Carolingian empire. The clarity and ease of writing made this script a long-lasting and popular hand. Today, it is the script I recommend students work on mastering first as it teaches a great deal of control and strong foundational skills.

The characteristic long ascenders with their distinctive serifs and overall rounded forms distinguish Carolingian from other contemporary hands. There are several variations which can be found through numerous manuscripts, but the overall visual character is fairly consistent. This hand is lettered at 3 to 5 pen widths in height for the x-height. The ascenders and descenders should be penned at the same height as the x-height.

Carolingian Ductus

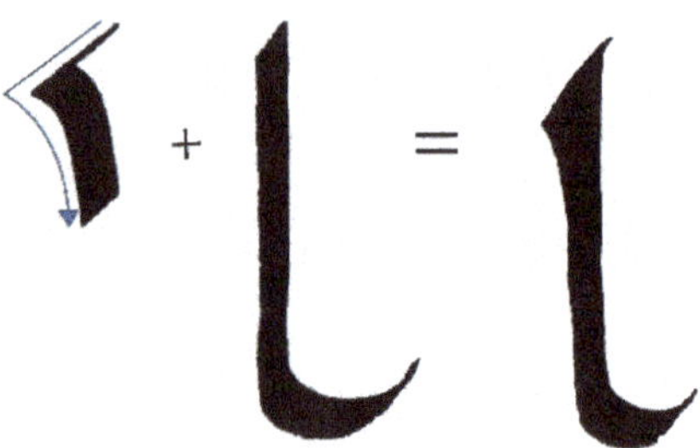

First and foremost, we have to examine the serif as it is one of the quintessential elements which set Carolingian apart. It begins with the long vertical stroke having already been performed. Placing the pen along the upper angle of the stroke, slide the nib to the left then arc it downwards meeting the vertical staff neatly about 1/3 the way from the top. This stroke can be concave, as shown, or it may be slightly convex and club-like. Both are considered acceptable and have been seen in period manuscripts. Practice the serif until it is consistent throughout. It will add a lot of beautiful texture to a document written in this hand.

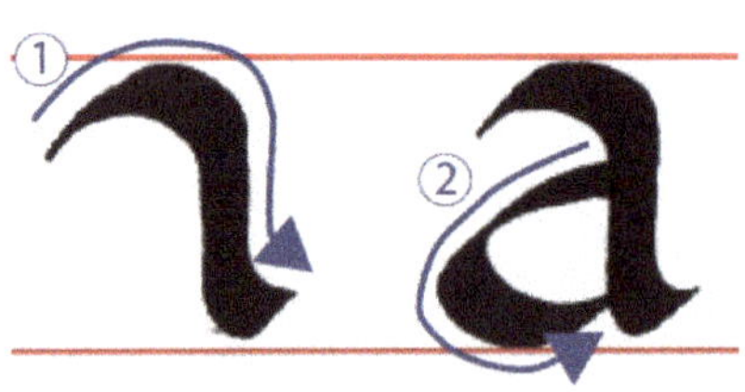

The A is a relatively simple two-stroke letter. The difficulty in forming the A comes on the second stroke as you are pushing the nib rather than pulling it. Just go slow and use a little less pressure than you think you might need. Otherwise, you run the risk of digging into the page and/or splattering ink. Those pushing strokes will become second nature in no time give plenty of practice. So, practice!

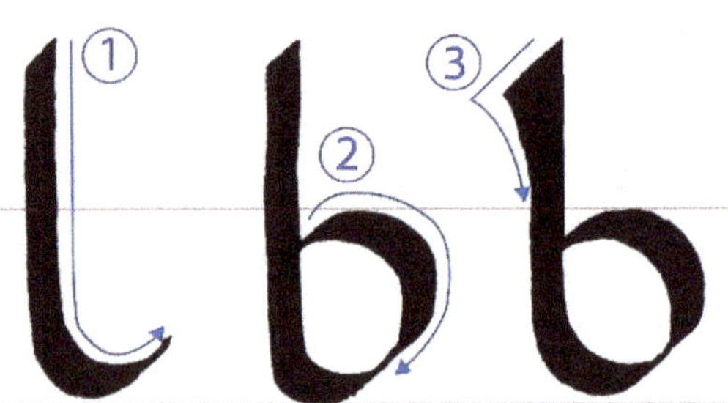

The B is a great example of a letter embodying many of the common strokes used throughout the rest of the Carolingian hand. Keep the ascender nice and straight until it bends gracefully to the baseline starting approximately 4/5 of the way down. Make certain you leave a thin hairline into which the second stroke can attach. Give it a classy serif and you're on your way to mastering another letter, Have I mentioned that you're doing a terrific job?

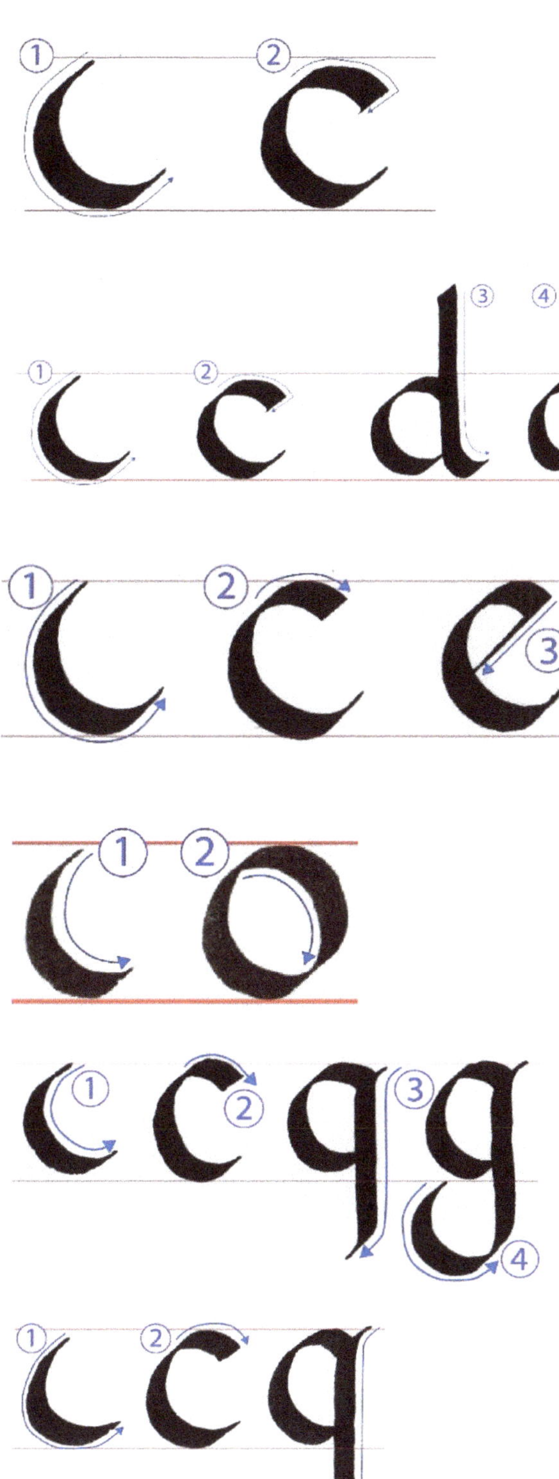

The basic form of the letter C also forms the basis of D, E, G, O, and Q. There are just a few minor details separating them. Overall, try to maintain constant curves to maintain the round shape of the letters.

G and Q follow a similar pattern to the C at the outset. Their descenders, of course, mark their differences.

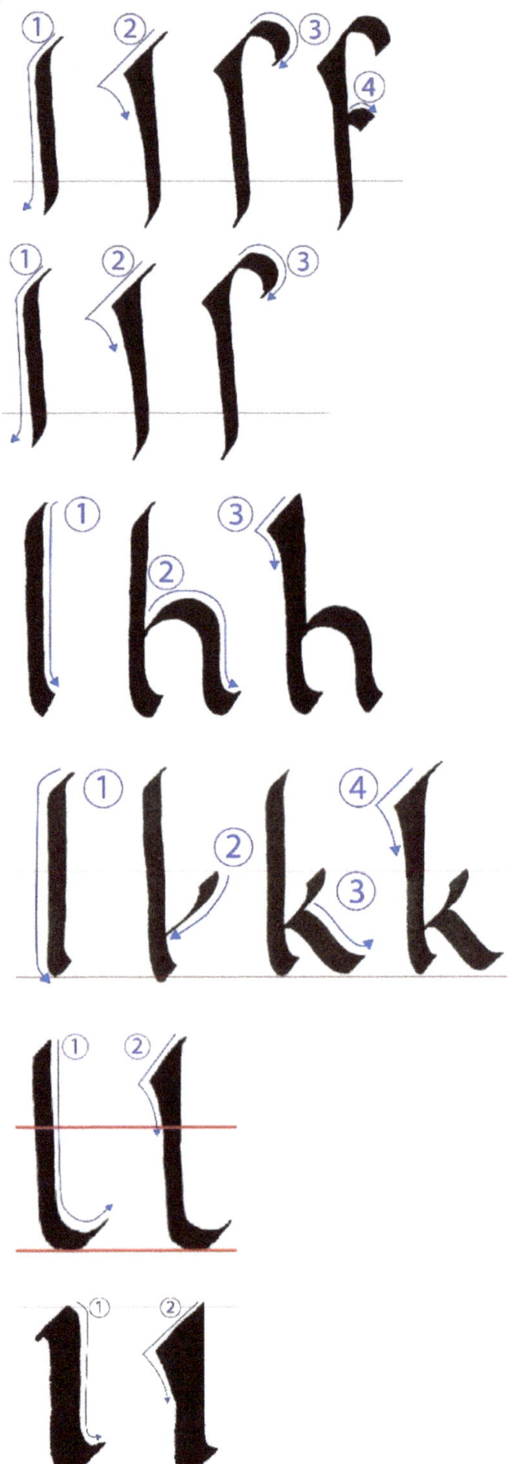

The F and the long-S (used in the beginning and middle of words, not as a final letter, generally) share an identical construction save for F's middle stroke. They both share the distinction of being semi-ascenders and semi-descenders, existing in some intermediate dimension.

Let's round out the rest of the ascenders with H, K, and L. Similar in construction but each, of course, varies significantly in the final strokes. Mind the serifs!

The I and the J, too, are similarly constructed. Keep the vertical strokes nice and straight until the very end, then give each a little curve. The J should end in a trailing point, of course. Top them off with the serif and

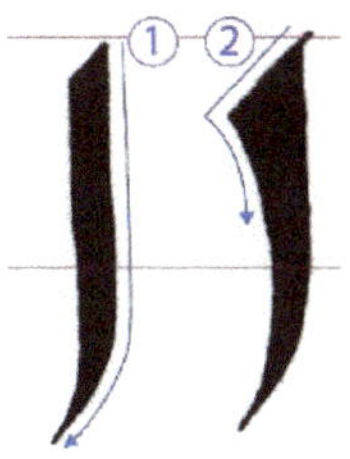

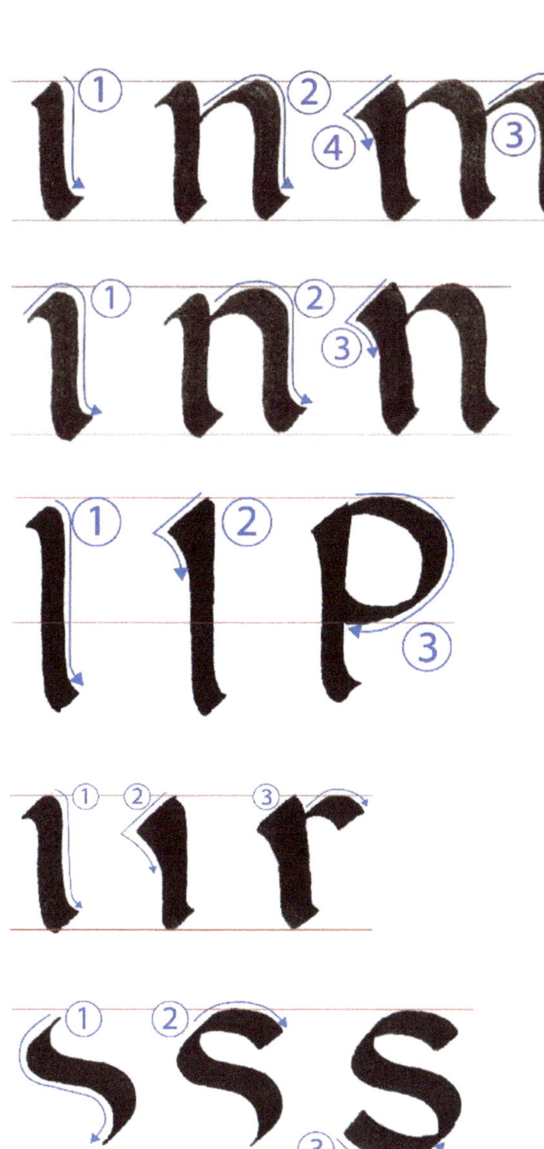

feel free to dot the letters or not, it is your choice. Both variants are seen in medieval manuscripts, so whether the undotted letters were stylistic or simply the result of a lazy scribe, we may never truly know. If all else fails and someone calls you out on the absence of jots and tittles in your work: blame it on Titivillus; that dirty little imp!

The M and the N should have refined, fair curves. The negative space between the strokes should be 2-times the vertical stroke width. Don't forget the serif, even in the x-height letters.

At this point, the P should be easy-peasy for you. The descender starts at minim height, stays vertical on its route, stopping with a slight forward kick. Finish the descender off with the standard serif before giving the letter a nice, round belly.

If you can make an I, then you are well on your way to making the R. After all, it's just an I sticking it's tongue out! Make sure there is a nice curve on the 'tongue'.

The first stroke of the S starts and stops just shy of the minim line and the baseline. Take your time in forming the curves and making certain the second and third strokes connect neatly with the initial stroke.

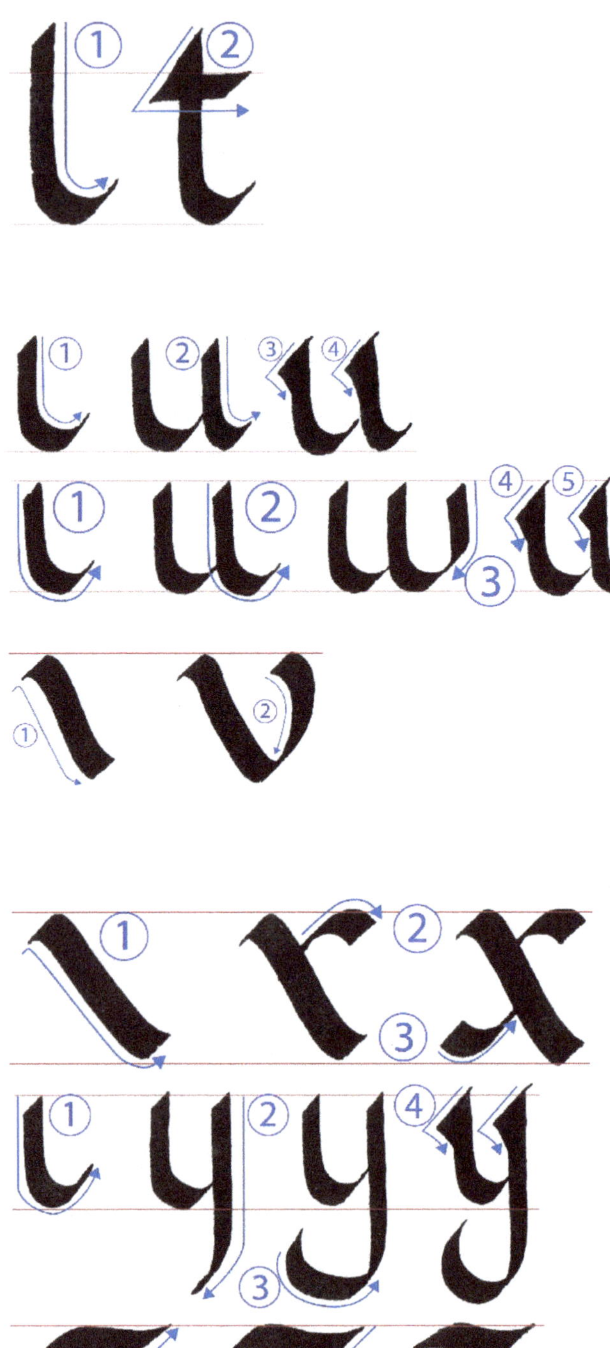

The T just barely reaches above the x-height line at the start of the descending stroke. A nice curve finished off by a hairline completes the descender. Match the angle of the top of the descender to begin forming the cross which should sit just under the x-height line.

Start just under the minim line for the U with two matched descenders. A matched set of serifs will finish it off perfectly.

The W is similar to the U save for the third stroke terminates into the end of the second stroke.

V starts with a simple, angular stroke from the minim line to the baseline. A lightly curving second stroke finishes the letter off. Slight hairline strokes can be used at the start of both strokes to add additional character if desired.

The champion of the x-height is, of course, the X! Fine hairlines add a bit of grace to the start and finish of the initial stroke. The second and third strokes should curve in gracefully.

Y should be very graceful. The third stroke can lay flatter beneath the baseline or curve slightly upwards.

While Z is shown here using three strokes for its construction, it is frequently done in single, combined stroke.

PROJECT 3: I SHALL BE CALLED

If you haven't done it already, set up a practice sheet and write your name. Write it a few times. Write your significant other's name, your children's names. Go wild!

Now, try it in different colors, different sizes, and on different paper. Pick your very favorite version and hang it on your refrigerator. Good work!

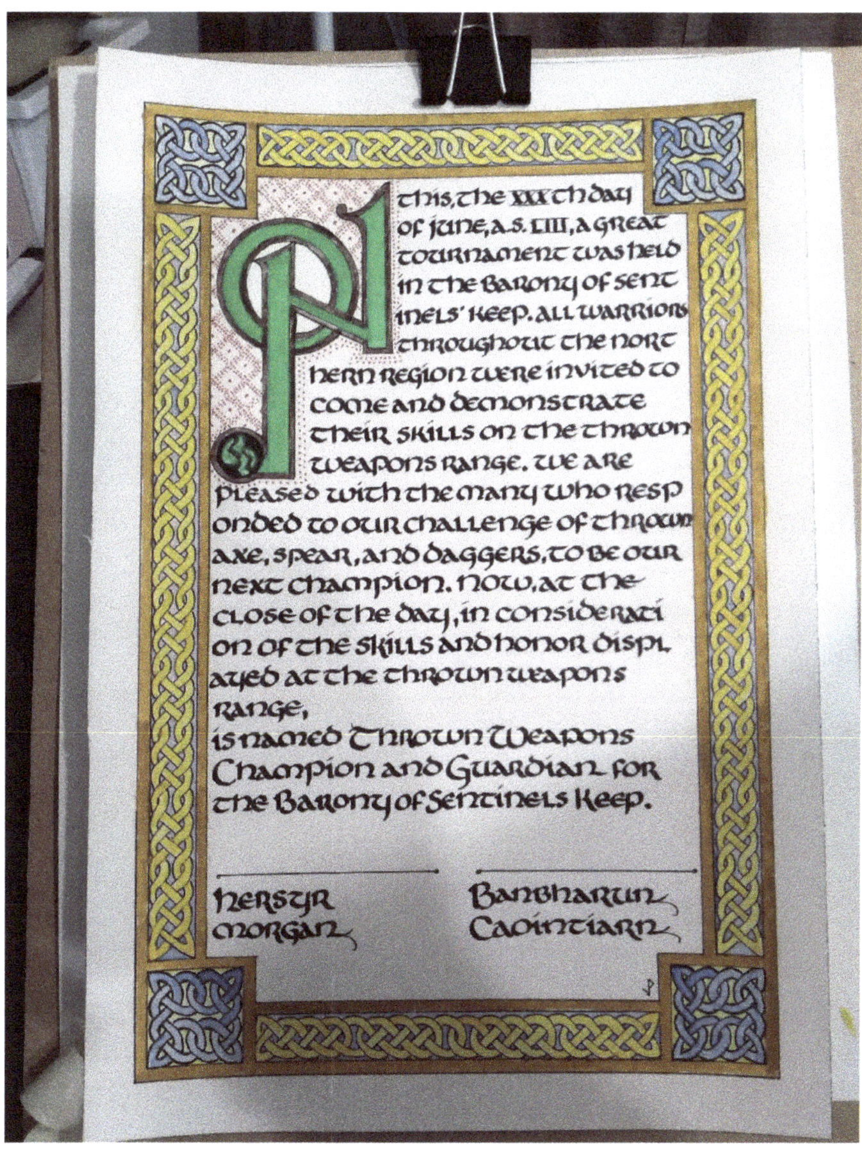

VIII. GOTHIC TEXTURA QUADRATA

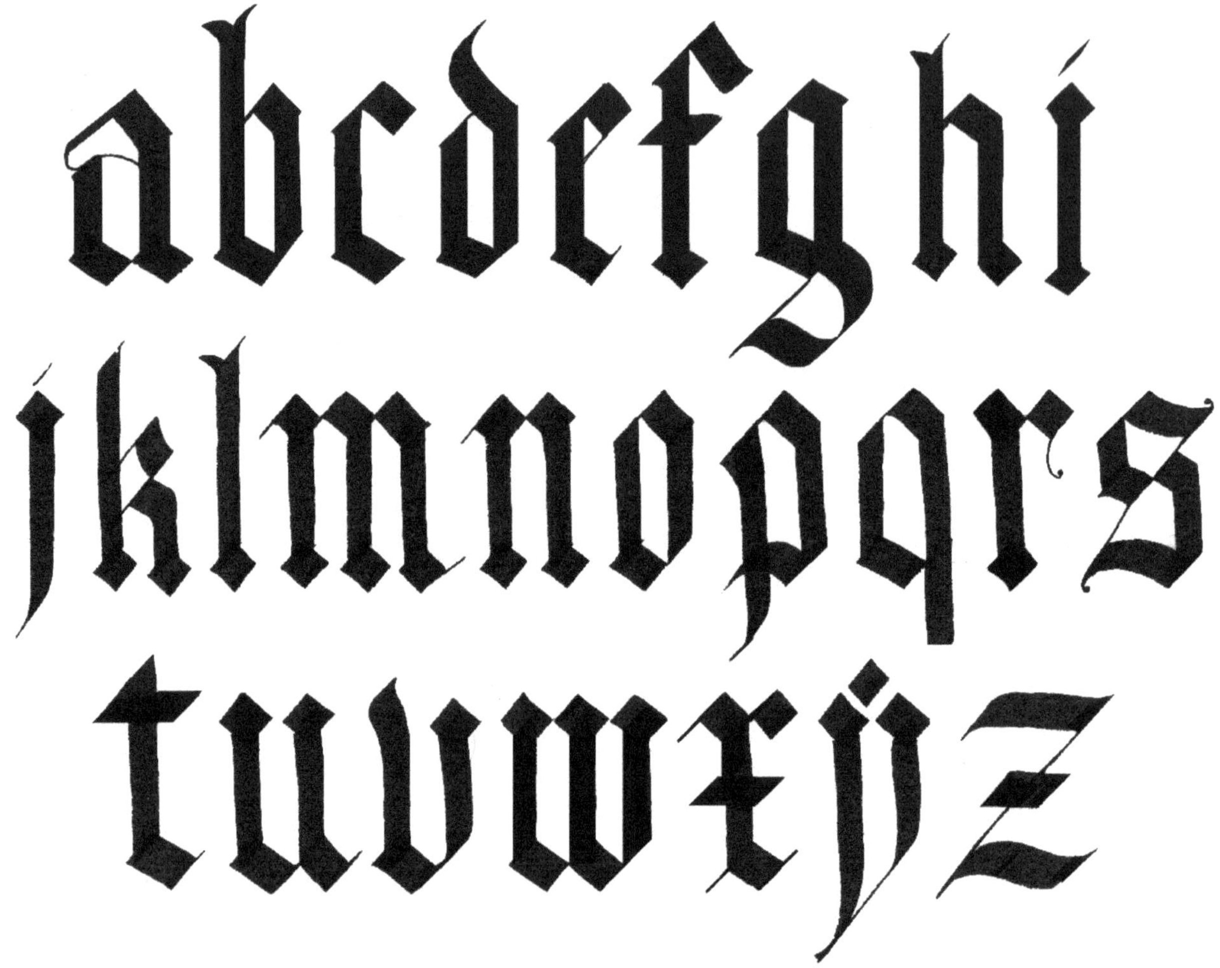

Figure 21 - Gothic Textura Quadrata Exemplar

Gothic Textura Quadrata was in use from the 1200s through the late 1400s CE. It was thought to be more readable due to the boldness of the condensed letterforms. The vertical structure, rectangular shape, and rigidity of the letters are said to resemble the texture of fabric on the page.

Letter height can vary between 3 to 5 pen widths for the base height and the pen angle, too, can vary from 30° to 45°. The 'diamonds' on the vertical strokes should be centered and symmetrical inasmuch as it is possible. Take your time when writing in this script; your patience will be rewarded. Use vertical guidelines to assist you when learning Textura Quadrata. You are only limited by how many lines you're willing to erase in the end!

There are a number of people who have confessed to me that their biggest problems with Gothic Textura Quadrata are getting consistent line spacing and straight strokes. My

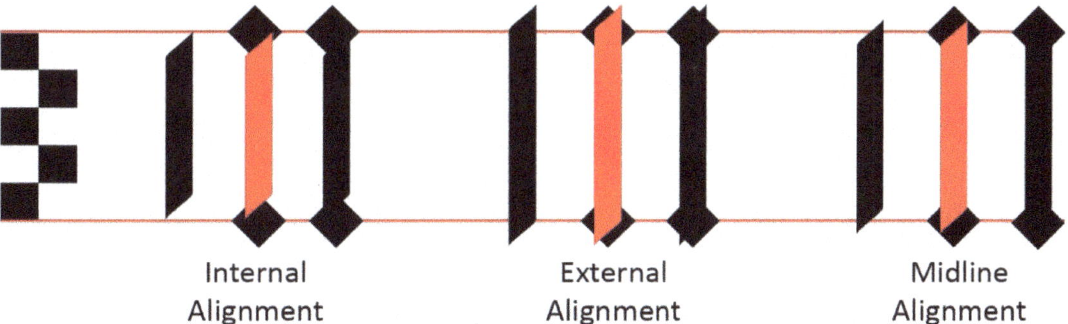

Figure 22 - Alignment of Vertical Strokes Relative to Guidelines

suggestion for this is to simply perform the verticals first, then come back and finish off with the diamonds or other major strokes, then finally any hairlines and ornamental strokes.

It should be noted, of course, that there are some alignment issues that one must be aware of when constructing the vertical strokes in relationship to the diamonds and the guidelines. Figure 22 demonstrates the possible alignments of the strokes to the guidelines and the resulting appearance. In most cases, a midline alignment is preferred to avoid indents or long tails from appearing. Figure 23 on the other hand indicates that a slightly longer internal alignment, at the end of a vertical which will receive an oblong stroke, is optimal. Practice and experience will lead you to what works best for you.

It should be noted that capital versions of Gothic Textura Quadrata did exist in the medieval period. The use of versals (decorated, large uncial variations) were, however, far more commonly employed. I would encourage you to look into various other resources if you are interested in seeing the wide variety of capitals you can press into service.

Furthermore, you should know that there are many variations of Gothic Textura Quadrata that have been used throughout the Middle Ages. Examining period examples is

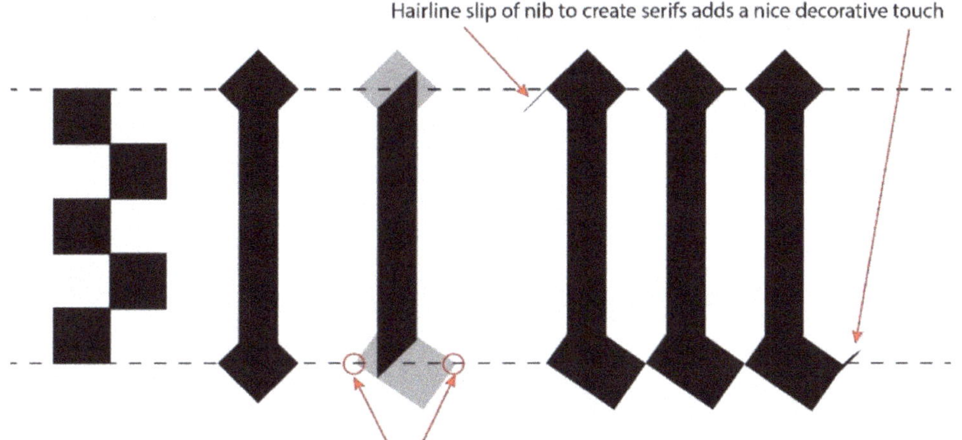

Figure 23 - Alignment of Diamonds Relative to Guidelines

the best method of familiarizing yourself with them. Modern textbooks, like this one, lack the scope to give a comprehensive survey.

Gothic Textura Quadrata Ductus

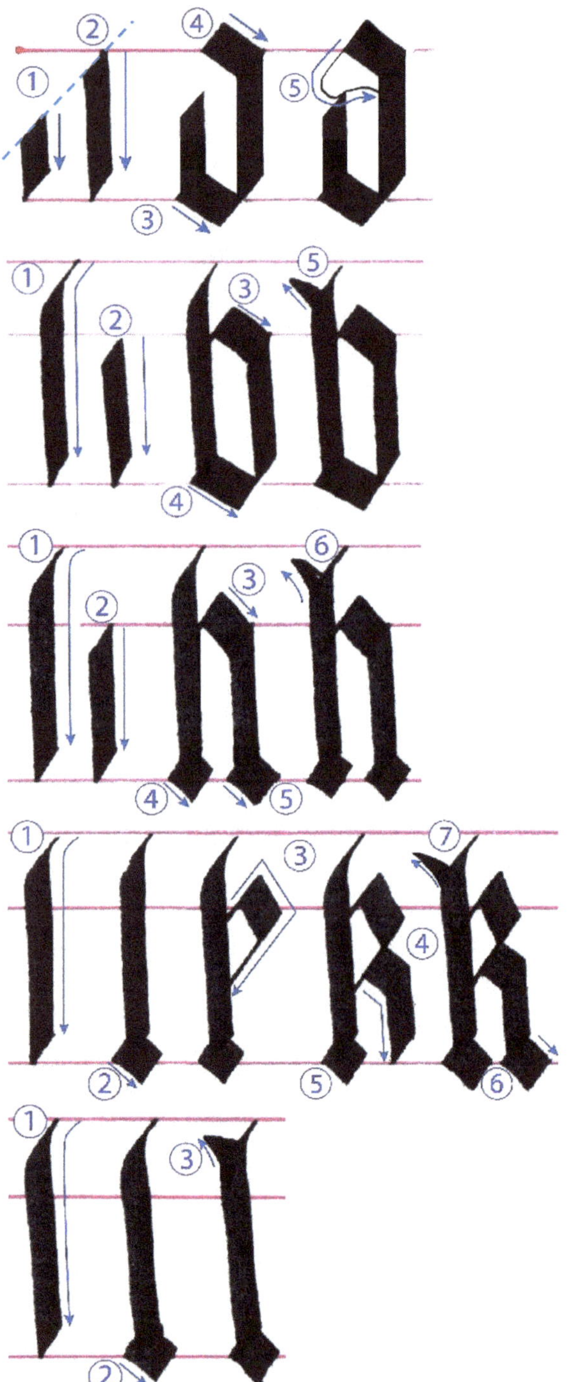

The A differs from the C and O in that the initial stroke is slightly less than 2/3 the x-height. Ideally, you should be able to visualize a line through the angles of the tops of the vertical strokes. For the 5th stroke, use the inside corner of your nib.

The B, H K, and L are grouped together primarily because they are ascenders with the hooked serif. This is accomplished by either using the inside corner of your nib to pull out the hook from the body of the serif or using a small nib afterwards to form it.

Make certain to slide into the vertical just slightly from the right. This forms a delicate hairline that is very attractive.

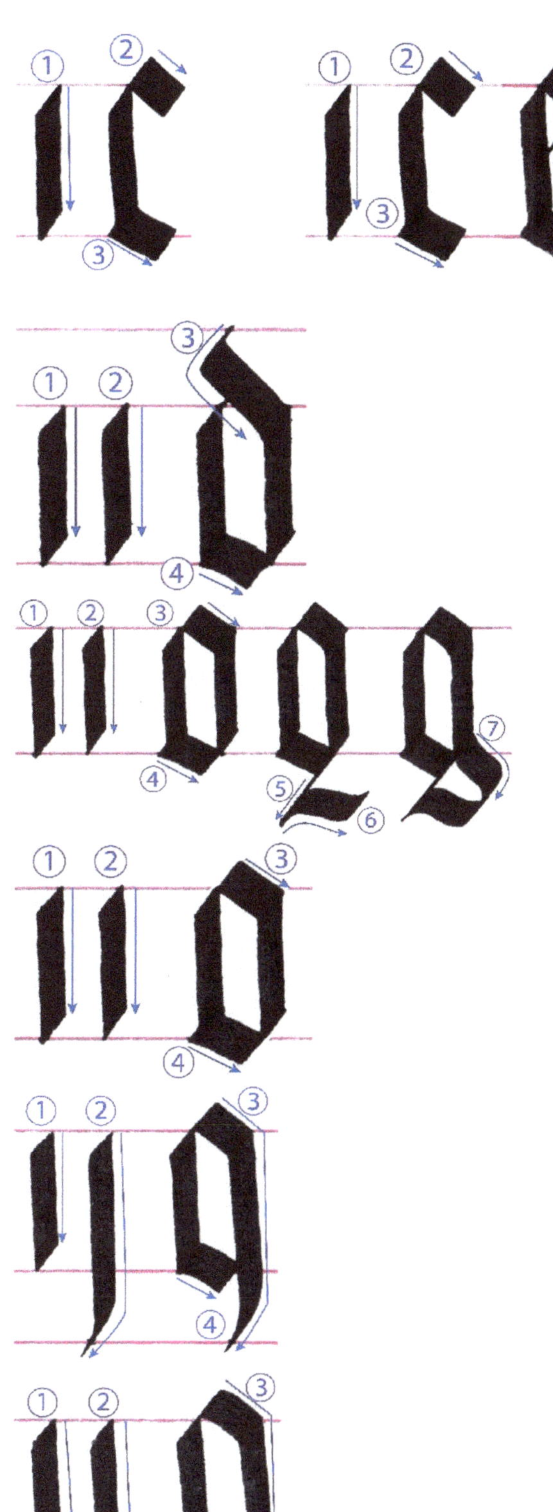

C and E differ only in the addition of the closing line in the 4th stroke. Try to keep the length and angle of the top and bottom strokes nearly identical for a balanced appearance.

Similar to O, the D, G, Q, and P share a very similar profile. It is the quadrilateral shape that gives this hand its titular characteristic.

G's curves require a little work to perfect. Just keep practicing it. If you are diligent and pay close attention, you will find your aha-moment!

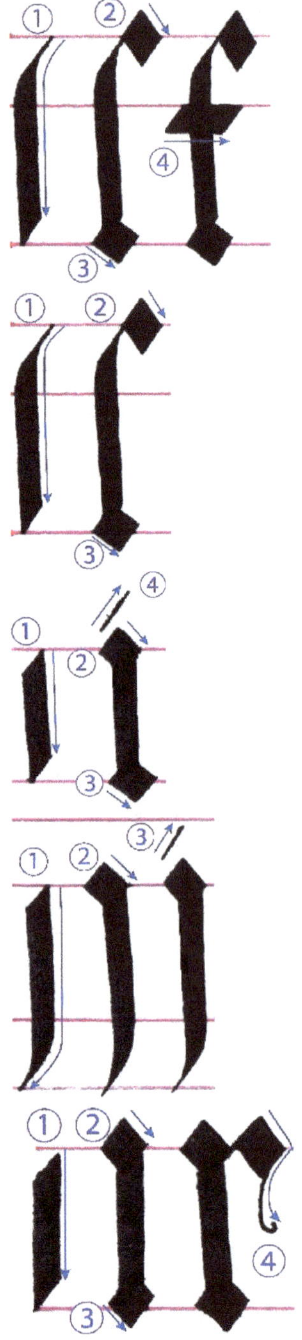

F and long-S are also virtually identical save for the horizontal bar set just below the x-height line. You can add a decorative stroke to this line or even to the top stroke on the long-S if you would like; see the 4th stroke of the R for an example.

I, J, and R are constructed similarly; J just descends and terminates in a fine line. The tittle above the I and the J is simply a light stroke with the edge of your pen.

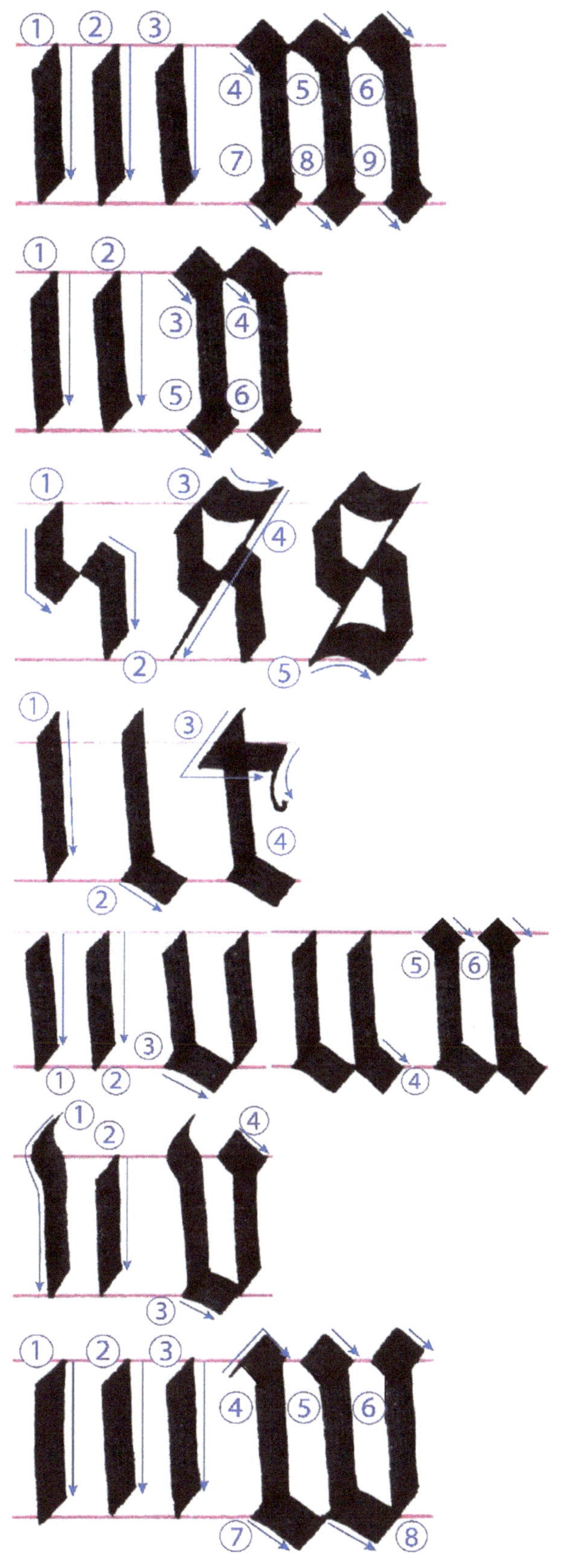

M and N require perfect spacing to not look gangly. The negative space between the strokes should be 1.25 to 1.5 times the width of the vertical strokes.

Take your time: the S has been the crux of learning Gothic Textura Quadrata for many a modern scribe.

T sits a little proud of the x-height line, but only about the width of a pen-nib. That decorative line on the fourth stroke is identical to what you used on the R and possibly F and long-S. Just use the corner of your nib to draw it.

U, V, and W also require the precise vertical spacing of M and N to look balanced.

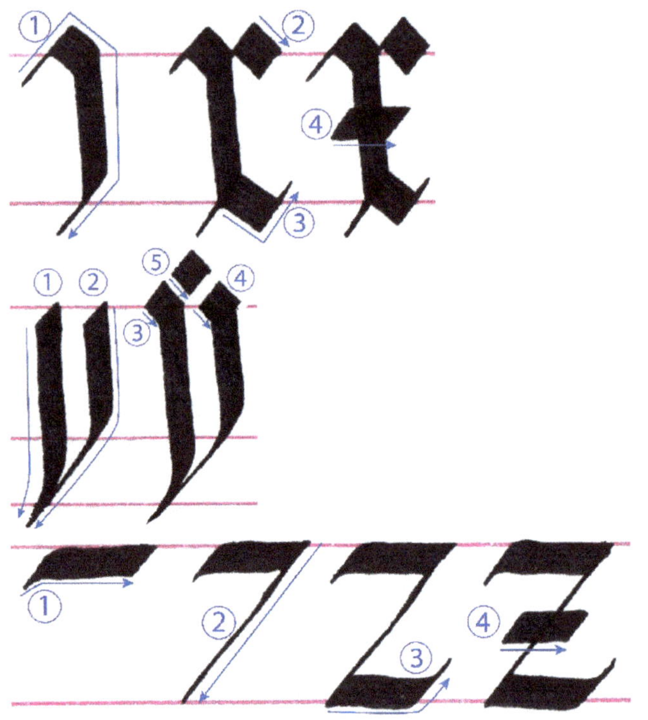

Yes, you must make certain to cross your X and give it a little foot, too!

While you're crossing your X, remember to dot your Y. Yes, seriously. It just looks right. You will see this variation frequently throughout the period when Gothic was prevalent.

I swear, I am not making this up! Cross your X, dot your Y, and cross your Z as well.

PROJECT 4: A ROSE BY ANY OTHER NAME

Using your favorite quote (or any random fun quote or poem), lay out a page and callig it! Use a large Uncial letter to start the quote, the rest of the text should be Carolingian or Gothic.

Bonus points: Use a different color ink for the initial Uncial letter and black for the rest of the text.

Double-bonus points: Decorate the paper with drawings related to the text. For example, Frost's "The Road Not Taken," I would decorate with oak leaves, acorns, and thistles. Have fun and take your time.

Congratulations! You can now say that you are a Calligrapher and Illuminator.

GLOSSARY

Ascender: Portions of letters that extend above the x-height line (b, d, h, l, k).

Baseline: The line on which the letters sit.

Broad-edged: A nib or marker with a chisel-edge profile.

Descender: Part of letters that extend below the baseline (g, j, p, q, y).

Hairline: The thinnest, finest stroke you can make with a pen.

Majuscule: Uppercase letter.

Minuscule: Lowercase letter.

Nib: The business end of a pen.

Serif: Decorative strokes which compose a portion of the first and last main strokes of a letter.

X-height: The height of the lowercase letters based on the letter x.

REFERENCES

Art, S. (n.d.). *Elegant Writer Family.* Speedball Art/Hunt Manufacturing Co. Retrieved December 22, 2020, from https://www.speedballart.com/our-product-lines/speedball-calligraphy-illustration/speedball-elegant-writer-markers/

Bischoff, B. (2012). *Latin Paleography: Antiquity & The Middle Ages.* (D. Ó. Ganz, Trans.) New York: Cambridge University Press.

Brown, M. P. (2018). *Understanding Illuminated Manuscripts: A Guide to Technical Terms.* Los Angeles: Getty Publications.

Brown, M. P., & Lovett, P. (2015). *The Historical Source Book for Scribes.* Toronto: University of Toronto Press.

Cennini, C. d. (2019). *Il Libro dell'Arte.* (D. V. Thompson, Trans.) New York: Dover Publications, Inc.

Chesne, J. d., & Baildon, M. J. (1571). *A Book Containing Divers Sorts of Hands.*

Child, H. (Ed.). (1986). *The Calligraphers Handbook.* New York: Taplinger Publishing Company.

Dass, R. (1978). *Be Here Now.* New York City: Harmony Books.

De Hamel, C. (1992). *Medieval Craftsmen: Scribes and Illuminators.* Toronto: University of Toronto Press.

Derolez, A. (2012). *The Paleography of Gothic Manuscript Books From the Twelfth to the Early Sixteenth Century.* New York: Cambridge University Press.

Douglas, R. (1967). *Calligraphic Lettering with Wide Pen & Brush* (3rd ed.). New York: Watson-Guptill.

Drogin, M. (1980). *Medieval Calligraphy, Its History and Technique.* New York: Dover Publications, Inc.

Furber, A. (1984). *Layout and Design for Calligraphers.* New York: Taplinger Publishing Co., Inc.

Hoffberg, Janet; Kastin, Judy; Fink, J.C.; Cooper, Maura. (1991). *Speedball Textbook.* Hunt Manufacturing Co.

Kipphan, H. (2001). *Handbook of Print Media: Technologies and Production Methods.* Springer.

Lovette, P. (2017). *The Art and History of Calligraphy.* London: The British Library.

Mayer, R. (1991). *The Artist's Handbook of Materials and Techniques.* New York: Penguin Books.

Merriam-Webster. (2020, December 30). Retrieved from Merriam-Webster.com Dictionary: https://www.merriam-webster.com/dictionary

Parish, J. (2006). *Magnificat.* Personal Collection, Butte.

Theophilus. (1979). *On Divers Arts.* (Hawthorne/Smith, Trans.) Dover Publications, Inc.

Thompson, D. V. (2018). *The Material and Techniques of Medieval Painting.* New York: Dover Publications, Inc.

Travers, C. (2016). *Beginning Illumination: Learning the Art, Step by Step.* Atglen: Schiffer Publishing, Ltd.

Wilson, D. H. (1990). *The Encyclopedia of Calligraphy Techniques.* Philadelphia: Running Press Book Publishers.

Wotzkow. (1967). *The Art of Hand Lettering.* New York: Dover Publications, Inc.

APPENDIX 1: DEALERS

John Neal Books

1833 Spring Garden Street, First Floor
Greensboro, NC 27403
Phone: 800-369-959
www.johnnealbooks.com

Paper and Ink Arts

113 Graylynn Drive
Nashville, TN 37214
Phone: 800-736-7772
www.paperinkarts.com

Dick Blick Art Materials

P.O. Box 1267
Galesburg, IL 61402-1267
Phone: 800-828-4548
www.dickblick.com

Pergamena

Phone: 845-457-3834
www.pergamena.net

Cass Art

Phone: +44 (0) 20 7619 2601
www.cassart.co.uk

L. Cornelissen & Son

105 Great Russell Street
London, UK WC1B 3RY
Phone: +44 (0) 20 7636 3655
www.cornelissen.com

Penman Direct

Phone: +44 (0) 19 5354 8770
www.penmandirect.co.uk

APPENDIX 2: PRACTICE WORKSHEETS

On the following pages, you will find a number of practice worksheets that you may photocopy at will for your personal use. A quadrille pad or other similar grid paper can also be used but you must test your ink on each paper for bleeding. Some paper and ink combinations just don't work! The only way to know, however, is to test all the variations and keep records.

1.5mm Nib x 3 Nib-Width Practice Sheet

1.5mm Nib x 4 Nib-Width Practice Sheet

2mm Nib x 3 Nib-Width Practice Sheet

2mm Nib x 4 Nib-Width Practice Sheet

2mm Nib x 5 Nib Width Practice Sheet

3mm Nib x 3 Nib Width Practice Sheet

3mm Nib x 4 Nib Width Practice Sheet

3mm Nib x 5 Nib Width Practice Sheet

4mm Nib x 3 Nib Width Practice Sheet

4mm Nib x 4 Nib Width Practice Sheet

4mm Nib x 5 Nib Width Practice Sheet

5mm Nib x 4 Nib Width Practice Sheet

5mm Nib x 5 Nib Width Practice Sheet

INDEX